Popular Capitalism

by

C. P. Klapper

Also by C. P. Klapper

~

The Washington Poems
Sonnets for the Spanish
The Fallacies of Atheism

Popular Capitalism

by
C. P. Klapper

The Lion and Lambda Press
New Brunswick, New Jersey

Copyright © 1986, 2013 by Carl Peter Klapper.

All Rights Reserved. No part of this book may be reproduced, stored in a retrieval system or transmitted in any form or by any means without the permission of the publisher.

First Edition, 1986, Unpublished Copyrighted.

Second Edition, 2013, Paperback. Elaborated, Revised.

ISBN-13: 978-1-934882-02-3 (paperback)
Library of Congress Control Number: 2013915246

Printed in the United States of America.

Dedication

To my Dad, who was curious about every topic and fascinated with populism after a Boy Scout trip to Washington where he got an "Every Man a King" pin from Huey Long,

To my Mom, who is equally curious and eager to share the wisdom of her grandparents' Swedish homeland in its Middle Way and love of peace,

To my brother Rich, who encouraged my interest in political economics and was always ready for a spirited discussion or debate,

and

To my friend, Gordie Cole, with whom I could discuss these weighty matters as comfortably and as easily as critiquing a Redskins game at the office and who would regale me with wonderful stories about Huey Long.

Preface to the Second Edition

In returning to this book after a space of more than twenty years, I fully expected that I would have to completely rewrite the old text as well as augment it with a more complete rendering of its original vision. Imagine my delight, then, that so much of the original wording not only reads better than I remember, but expresses themes and ideas with which I still agree. This is all the more surprising since, I must confess, the first edition was a hastily written and brief exposition of a few core ideas for which I wanted some credit and the recognition of my right to expand upon later.

Even so, this edition will restructure and reformat the original with its augmentations into a new and expanded list of chapters. It is my hope that this aids the comprehension of my argument for and description of what I believe to be a more productive and rational form of political economy. From that hope springs the further wish that legislators will enact laws and directives that bring my best ideas to life. If that wish comes true, I would then dream that the realization of those ideas truly benefit my neighbors and fellow citizens, both in the ways I intended — to end poverty and to allow the people to achieve their individual and corporate destinies — and through blessings I did not and could not expect.

Carl Peter Klapper
Christmas 2012
Metuchen, NJ

Table of Contents

Preface to the Second Edition.................... vii

A Limited Goal.. 3

The Cost of Sovereignty............................. 7

The Suggestion... 25

The Provision.. 45

The Funding.. 69

The Polis and the Oikos............................. 105

The College... 117

The Village.. 149

Popular Capital... 185

Urban Federalism....................................... 247

The Bank and Exchange............................ 297

The Treasuries, Trade, Aid and War.......... 313

Response to Possible Objections............... 367

Call to Inaction... 389

A Limited Goal

A Limited Goal

I give a gift of policy. Decide its value as you will. This gift of policy will not be a plan for Utopia[1]. The flaws of Man and the variety of Nature are sufficient to wreck any such plan and its grand hopes. It would be no gift to mislead the people into expecting the impossible and then to give them yet another disaster.

Rather, I will give only an improvement, fulfilling modest hopes. Once achieved, we can again survey the scene and find what more should be done. Others may like to place their hopes for a better world on the organization of their political economy. Such is not the source for my hope, though I believe some good might be done by better policy or, at least, less harm.

Yet many keep their partisan political hope to the exclusion of decency and kindness and all which

---
1 See [MORE] for the misunderstood original.

might embarrass their rabid anger against the *status quo*. Thus they adopt one or another of the current ideals, making others miserable while they fight for it.

Not wanting to make my own theories a cause of misery, I prohibit all who read this book from adopting its proposals as dogma, from ceasing to criticize its reasoning and from hesitating to offer alternatives. Mind that I have no desire to handicap my philosophy, already laboring under the obscurity of its author, so I urge that the same attitude be taken towards the writings of all political philosophers and the current mode of living, however famed or adored. The present landscape is scarred and littered with the assumptions and obsessions of the past. We should not hesitate from clearing the land for more fruitful use on account of its more recent accretions of concrete and plasterboard.

Before making a suggestion, I will first consider the costs which all political economies must face. Any realistic policy must, of course, deal with these costs, if they are to be put into practice. I will go further, though, making this the main subject of my improvement, from which all else is elaboration and enhancement.

The Cost of Sovereignty

The Cost of Sovereignty

There is no inherent right to rule. History has long since dismissed any delusions of such a right, whether bestowed by religion or by society or by science or by mythic tribe made god. Rather, the right to rule, sovereignty, must be bought from those who are ruled. In economic terms, any dominant entity which rules must pay the opportunity cost of its own sovereignty, this being the best perceived benefit from the available alternatives, including anarchy. Since each prospective or current subject would assume that they would survive in anarchy, which is always individually available, the cost of sovereignty over each individual is at least the cost of survival. However, it has sadly been the practice of rulers to cheat individuals out of their due and instead deal with the aggregate.

To understand how this dodge is effected without general anarchy ensuing, we will first consider what exactly the predominant entity is. We should not limit our view of its scope, lest we neglect the power behind the throne, allowing it to avoid our analysis in the mists of assumption and unexamined certainty. Thus, we broadly define the predominant entity for a country as the system whereby most powers are created, transferred, retained and destroyed. Calling this power system by its more traditional name, *political economy*, reminds us that power may come as much from money and markets as from government and laws, that wealth may come as much from politics as from commerce.

A *political economy* is thus a system of creating, transferring, retaining and destroying power which is not only accepted, but is the predominant system for these transactions. If something merely inspires a few highly visible transactions of power, then it can not properly be called a *political economy*, but a plan, ideology, or wish for a *political economy*. Some other power system supplies the process actually in force; and it is the real *political economy*. Therefore, in order to establish itself as a *political economy*, a power system must first gain that acceptance and predominant use for transactions of political and economic power.

The power system that gains that predominance need not be a monolith or controlled by a monolithic institution or power. It is sufficient that the political economy operate by the rule of law, whether based on informal convention or on a formal constitution, enforced by a judicial system or the threat of revolt, with multiple actors, major or minor, coordinating their parts in adherence to that law. Indeed, it seems that most political economies operate in just such a complex manner, where competing ruling powers are balanced. There is good reason for this. If the power system is nearly impossible for any one person or group to control, the prospect of it being corrupted to serve the special interests of that person or group is also unlikely. Then the people can have some degree of confidence that the political economy, where it touches their lives most intimately, is not completely rigged for the benefit of those special interests, and they will be more willing to abide by the resulting distribution of power.

Returning again to the tasks of the political economy, the creation, destruction, retention and transfer of power, let us next consider, with some generality, how it might achieve these tasks. In so doing, my intention is not to specify the exact mechanism, but to point out where we might be assuming to be inviolable, natural and permanent, what are the fragile products of sovereignty. Only then can we determine the costs of that sovereignty and more rationally and efficiently assign their payment.

The creation of power consists of creating property and positions of authority. Hard though it may be for us sometimes to fathom, the land we claim as property today was once not owned by any person, and all of the political positions to which people hope to get elected had their first year of existence. Grants were made and constitutions ratified by a power system of some time ago creating those powers. Even today, laws create property in arenas built by telecommunications, just as laws have created property in skyscrapers built by engineering. Every new business is a created power, as is every new government agency. To say that we own something or that we hold an office then presupposes that the power to own that thing or to hold that office have been validly created or re-created. That validity is, in turn, based on the sovereignty vested in the political economy which has created those powers, at the time of their creation, as well as the sovereignty vested in each political economy with jurisdiction over those powers from then until now. If these political economies have not paid the costs of their sovereignty, the properties and political positions over which power or ownership is claimed are themselves then called into question. Why should this condominium or website be owned? Why should there be a President of our republic?

The same applies to the destruction of powers, except that it only takes the sovereignty of the present to destroy long-standing powers. This is because this destruction of powers is a step towards the anarchic alternative to powers. Therefore, there is nothing taken away from the public when powers are destroyed, but something given back for its benefit now, without reference to precedents. Who held something long ago then ceases to be relevant. What matters is now: Who is holding it now? Who are the people living in this home, this town, this country today? Anything which goes against this temporary, fluid and anarchic possession, must have far greater validity and acceptance than its nine-tenths of the law. If a power lacks authority for a moment, it is refuted indefinitely. There is no vacuum, but a change from property and station into domain.

The retention of power is more familiar to us in the various phrases we use to assert them. When that power is economic, we know it as *property rights*. When it is political at its widest public scope, we call it *national security*. There are variations: retention of partisan power in *the two-party system*, the vestigial claims from ghosts of precedents and ancient treaties, and assurances that an elected official can hold their office until the next election unless removed by a legally sanctioned procedure. In all of these, power is retained not by right, but by acquiescence or force. Any claim that the first responsibilities of government are the protection of private property and national defense, assumes that government rightfully holds the authority to bear those responsibilities. If the political economy, of which the government is a part and an agent, has not paid the cost of sovereignty, then that government has no right to exist or to perform its sovereign functions, including the protection of private property, military defense, the collection of revenue and the continuance of any elected office. Repression and the deceit of calls for patriotic duty then add to the cost of sovereignty, placing its burden on the people rather than the rulers.

It is not only in the tools of repression and patriotism that the cost of maintaining a political economy is increased by them, for the transfer of power must be prefaced by a decision to transfer that power. Indeed, any political economy, in administering power transfers, must involve itself not only with the process of transferring power, but also with the decision process of that transfer so that these involvements are also based on sovereignty. Thus, in the political sphere, both elections and inaugurations are tasks whose legitimacy presupposes that the cost of sovereignty have been paid. In the economic world, in each market, the processes of trading and of settlement, as well as the control of the money used in these processes, are rightfully ruled by the political economy when and only when the cost of sovereignty has been paid. If it has not been paid, who is to say that coups and piracy, ballot frauds and counterfeiting are objectionable? Preventing these are then an additional cost of establishing the political economy.

Indeed, every institution which is considered an inviolable cornerstone of our civilization and based on the sovereignty of the political economy can be swept away in a blink of an eye if that sovereignty is dismissed. The failure to pay the cost of sovereignty, by calling into question the sovereignty of the political economy, places that power system in peril of being dismissed and its institutions of being dismantled. Seeing the wide scope of consequences and all that is at stake, we can better understand the extreme measures taken to manipulate that cost to ensure it is paid by or, rather, extracted from the people.

We can also conclude from the foregoing that the cost of sovereignty over the people as an aggregate, living their lives within the confines of the institutions, governance and laws of a political economy, is the cost incurred by that political economy in establishing an authority for its institutions, its governance and its laws in the face of the cost of sovereignty over each individual. This authority may be established in a number of ways. However, it is practically impossible to achieve that authority without some cooperation from the people. Is government to move every arm and leg of the people? The more brutal governments may use intimidation and fear to gain authority, but the people at least oblige to be afraid. More often, people just decline to resist, if that is possible. Yet, every now and then, people resist most fiercely and seem to discard their former timidity.

We would remain confused at this phenomenon if we insisted on viewing the people as a group with a common persona. However, people are a mixed bag, in timidity as in other characteristics. Those who decline to resist the government, moreover, do so for a number of reasons beside timidity: patriotism, endorsement of the government's policy, apathy, peacefulness and love, among others. The result is a spectrum of personalities, covering every conceivable degree of inclination to resist the establishment of authority. When those who are less inclined to resist are predominant, then there is peace, which influences many marginal cases towards peacefulness: the people seem meek.

Resistance, on the other hand, can take many forms depending on the inclinations of its leaders and those marginal cases open to their leadership or suasion. When the violent are ascendant, so is violence and thus the marginal cases resort to arms at inconvenient times. When cheaters are ascendant, some marginal cases cheat on the margins. When those who refuse are ascendant, some marginal cases become lazy when ordered. When those who ignore are ascendant, some marginal cases claim not to understand the language of the officers of the political economy. The people in this case are not being corrupted by poverty or other ills, but are resisting their oppression in a matter consistent with their demographics. The demographics then assure a continued resistance which eventually undermines and destroys the political economy.

One way to not let demographics control you is for you to control demographics. There is no need here for some elaborate procedure using the latest technology. Rather, we need only appreciate the way that policies allow certain types of people to prosper while constraining others. The essential demographic aim of a political economy is the preponderance of those who follow its rules. This is what has to be achieved, by whatever method, if it is to establish its authority. In other words, the cost of achieving this goal is the cost of sovereignty.

Yet what happens when a political economy makes it hard for the people living by its rules to survive? Some of these will continue following those rules, even in poverty. The political economy, in this case, is fortunate to have virtuous citizens. If virtue has such costs, though, virtue starves and vice remains. Not a heart will be corrupted, but the community will have been corrupted by attrition. Punishment of the evil will not avail: if they are killed, the population shrinks until it vanishes; if not, there are more to punish or to create chaos. Either way, the political economy has not established its authority. It is necessary, therefore, that one can survive following the rules.

Viewed in another way, this is nothing more than the opportunity costs of obedience. If we allow people to do anything in a model, and this is what we do when we think demographically, letting one type replace another when the former is advantageous, then the cost of obedience is the value of what might otherwise be achieved. Since failure to survive moots other costs and benefits, the best action in disobedience is to at least assure survival. On the other hand, massive disobedience would make it likely that one could disobey the government and survive. Thus, the cost of obedience includes at least survival. Since obedience is the acceptance of authority, meeting the costs of obedience is the same as meeting the costs of sovereignty. Therefore, political economies must assure that the benefits of obedience include at least survival.

I do not claim that this necessity applies to governments. Sometimes the system does not dissolve immediately because the cost of authority is borne by the virtuous. Often, people are sustained by charity and other acts of kindness not required by the political economy. Alternatively, the costs can be met by economic rewards, employers paying the cost of sovereignty for their employees through their wages because it is mandated by law, because workers are organized into unions or because their work is worth more to the employer than the cost of survival for the employees. One way or another, though, the cost of survival must be paid or the system faces dissolution or depopulation.

The other cost of establishing a power system as a political economy is the cost of its operation, the cost of making transfers of power by its rules. This is determined by its nature. A power system which lets people exchange power as they wish, with only a few rules about this exchange, will cost less to operate than a system which tries to force and prohibit exchanges or one which controls them with stringent rules. We are not talking here of the degree of cooperation these systems might face, but of the costs of functioning given the same degree of cooperation. In the first case, the free system, cooperative parties fulfill the rules painlessly, with no great change in their lives from when they decided to exchange to when they made their exchange, aside from the changes engendered by its terms, which, indeed, they mutually preferred to not making that exchange. In the second, the authoritarian system, at least one of the parties must be informed of their duty to exchange and then make whatever adjustments are needed for the unforeseen realignment of their powers. In the third, the regulatory system, both parties undergo whatever contortions the stringent rules require to make their exchange, or give up if these are too hard or are prohibitively expensive. In the two latter cases, then, the exchanging parties face costs which they would not in the first. Clearly, a system of free markets and free elections is the most efficient political economy in its cost of operation.

A political economy, however, cannot exist by meeting just one of these costs, the cost of authority or the cost of operation. In the case of markets, a subset of power systems, much has been written about the costs of exchange, being its operating cost, while assuming the cooperation of its actors with the rules of exchange. The conventional attitude has been that the market rules are just so: eternal verities established by nature. Even if we modify this view by conceding that these rules developed by trial and error, it does not make sense in the modern world. In an age where trade is a profitable game for a few and a rare and petty game for most, harsh rules can be easily accepted. But as the domain of the market expands, and refuge vanishes, then the cost of losing this grander game escalates. The *laissez-faire* attitude seems to be derived from the observation that the market system had almost no cost of establishing its authority when it was not the predominant authority: when the political economy was centered on the family farm and the artisan's home. As soon as the political economy shifted away from farm and home and toward the market, the legitimacy of the *laissez-faire* attitude disappeared because the cost of authority for the market increased with its growing predominance.

As with any other power system, one based on the market system must meet the twin costs of operation and authority before it can become a political economy. Any suggestion for policy should then heed these costs, for policies can only be brought into effect by actual political economies. My suggestion will go further and deal primarily with these costs. In this way, I will try to avoid the pitfalls of the many who would pay the cost of authority by increasing the cost of operation with regulations, taxes, collective bargaining and the like. The lower these costs are to the people, the easier it is for them to climb out of poverty and to avoid sinking back in.

The Suggestion

The Suggestion

I should first explain this emphasis on cost. There is the concern that a political economy be able to sustain itself in the face of the tragedies which come its way. If a political economy has high costs, it is dependent on perpetual and pervasive prosperity to pay its costs. This makes it inherently unstable, no matter how much prosperity it would seem to produce.

Yet some may choose to forgo this efficiency and stability for some *higher* purpose. The Socratic philosophers sought an ethical goal of the *best* state of the *best* people.[1] I do not. Instead of ethics, with its petty divisions into powerful *good* and powerless *bad*, my goal is to enable each person to become what they were meant to be, to do what they feel in the core of

---

1 See [PLATO] and [ARISTOTLE] for their imposition of ethics on politics.

their being they were meant to do and to leave that work as an enduring legacy which will bless their community for generations to come. Mine is thus a Populist dream, where the power to achieve one's destiny is given to the people, individually and without exception. It should be clear, then, that we should avoid any additional expense beyond what is necessary to establish the political economy and to facilitate our pursuit of destiny. And so we proceed.

In order to keep the operating costs of its power system low, I suggest a political economy with few rules for exchange, as mentioned before. To do this, though, we must avoid giving too much power to too few people, lest they usurp the power system and install their own, for their own ends. Since political power is the easiest way to concentrate power, with the least limitations on its abuse, it should be discouraged. Instead, power should be held widely, people in control of the things they have on their persons and in their homes. The law should keep the politically powerful from seizing those things and not be used as a pretext for forcing the people to relinquish their personal power to maintain or augment the political power of others.

Nor should the law be used to force some people to pay others except by a contract freely entered into by both parties. We need to honestly and dispassionately reconsider our legal mechanisms in light of the cost of sovereignty. If the legal rationale for exacting payment is the need to survive instead of as an impartial penalty for committing a crime, then the mechanism is wrongly directed. It then affixes responsibility for survival where it does not belong and allows government, where that responsibility does belong, to shirk it. What we are left with, then, is the raw aggression of one party against another. If that aggression rewards the legal aggressor in proportion to the resources of their victim, then it is tantamount to highway robbery. This is the case with *tort*, so we should not be satisfied with reforming it, any more than we would be satisfied with reforming highway robbery. We should, instead, abolish *tort*. It has no place in popular capitalism or, in fact, any form of civilization.

In the absence of legal aggression through tort, the just use of the law exacts, from those accused of physical aggression, temporary and limited loss of power when charged and permanent loss only when convicted. A criminal case under laws against acts of violence never feathers the nest of accusers; it never gives an incentive to lie, cheat and steal under the veil of justice. It serves only as a disincentive for perpetrators of physical aggression regardless of profit. From this purpose, we should not divert it.

If our underlying intent, however, is to prevent the abuse of great economic power, we ought to first question the accumulation of that power and the lack of sufficient restraints on its use. In other words, we should adopt the same approach of *checks and balances* used in the United States Constitution to prevent abuse of political power and apply it also to the sphere of economic power. The *checks* would thus be in laws and regulations governing the operation of public banks and companies, as well as in the limitation of ownership and operation of the public companies to the public they are intended to serve. The *balances* would be in the wealth of the people, individually and in their communities, by which they can avoid subjugation to other economic powers. Therefore, the political economy should not inhibit growth, even — indeed, especially — great growth in economic power for those who have the least, but encourage all to acquire the means to resist economic as well as political pressures. An index of its performance in this regard would be the percentage of independently wealthy people.

The index currently in vogue, that of income equality, is not merely inaccurate but destructive of its aim of economic freedom for the poor. The policy implementing this index of income equality, punitive surcharges on high incomes, heap up burdens on those poor whose successful efforts might otherwise have allowed them to escape poverty. Meanwhile, those who have already accumulated wealth — using it to establish entrenched economic power over the poor — are able to escape these taxes by making or showing little or no income. Not only does great wealth inequality remain with this tax on upward mobility — *the millionaire's tax* in newspeak — but is enhanced in its worst aspect, that of the economic subjugation of the people, especially of the poor and indebted.

This is, sadly, just one recent example of how ignoring the minimal costs of authority, the costs of survival described earlier, have worked against the end of widely distributed independent wealth and the goal of preserving and protecting the power of the people. When these costs have not been paid by governments, the misery induced by that neglect ceded great political power to the unions as they sought to have them paid in their bailiwick, the workplace. As a result, the costs were paid largely by the employers of low-value labor through higher wages, increasing their costs and reducing their profits, thus discouraging expansion in their industries and eventually bringing contraction, protection and unemployment.

Worse, great masses of the public acquired a sympathy for organizations whose success was based on the manipulation of markets and the threat of violence. Most strikes would be ineffective without threats against strike-breakers. Even if a strike is based on empathy for fellow workers, it is a threat to destroy a business and to ruin its owner. By fostering the notion that the employer is the enemy, these strikes make brutality the language of the people, create fairy tales about a workers' paradise and generally dispense with reason and cooperation as a way to solve problems. Also, unions are concentrated political power and thus a threat to the economic power of each citizen, including their own members. Indeed, they have complicated the forming of contracts, introducing inefficiencies and distortions, often causing the very unemployment they claim to combat.

When the costs of authority have been handled by governments, they have also been handled poorly. There have been entitlement schemes, burdened with a costly bureaucracy and taxing the efforts of the working poor, not to mention allowing corruption and abuse. There have been lending and insurance schemes, which governments have endorsed and in which they have then participated, that purport to make more affordable those goods or services necessary for living, such as housing and medical care, or necessary, under current circumstances, for making a decent living, such as a college education or an automobile, but have instead made unaffordable for all but the very rich.

In truth, schemes like long-term mortgages and college loans, and health and automobile insurance throw more short-term money at their target product or service, thus inflating the prices of those same goods and services. Any subsequent deflation from a future reduction in spending money is diffused among the rest of the universe of goods which the borrower or insured might have otherwise purchased instead of making loan or premium payments. Also, the corrective deflation, being incrementally postponed with each payment, makes a full deflation uncertain as the credit worthiness upon which the loan was made recedes into the past. The combination of near-term inflation and a distant and unlikely deflation assure a speculative inflation.

Higher prices are considered a safe bet, so an increasing portion of the people take that bet in taking on more debt. After all, they think, the economy is expanding as the higher prices in the targeted goods spur their production and the production of every good used in their manufacture, so the increased demand and wages for labor assure us that these debts will be easily repaid. Besides, if we don't buy those products now, we will be paying more for them later. Of such thinking, speculative bubbles are born. In this case, it is a speculative bubble we benignly call *the business cycle*. This expression makes our debt bubble sound as inevitable as the natural cycle of evaporation and condensation.

To explain this supposedly natural business cycle, we are told to look at consumer confidence, when what matters is loan confidence: the confidence of lenders to lend more money and the confidence of borrowers to borrow it. If the borrowers grow more cautious and start paying down their debt, they are not buying more goods or services. If the banks refuse more loan requests, those who made the requests will not have that money for buying goods or services. Conversely, if there is more loan confidence, consumers have more money to buy goods and services. The pep rally economics of building consumer confidence is beside the point when consumer behavior is driven by a speculative game of *dare*.

From this, we also see that the money supply, another indicator we are told to watch, is only a factor when it is money which is lent, in other words, *debt money*. On the other hand, money issued by fiat and spent by the government may distort demand and, if not adequately offset by money returned to the government in revenue, may produce inflation at its issuance. That inflation is neither certain in the near term nor linked to a possible deflation in the future. The money returned in revenue may, at the next moment, exceed expenditures so that prices would then deflate, offsetting and possibly overriding the previous inflation. Moreover, nothing in the fiat price inflation threatens a massive deflation at some time in the future through a loss in confidence. Fiat money price inflation is simply not speculative, yet we are led to fear it and the fiat money which has not been prevalent in the United States since the Civil War. This fear is fabricated from the sins of its distant cousin, debt money, to which it is related only by being potentially part of the money supply.

Further confusion and misdirection has been unleashed upon the public from it being customary to

The Suggestion

think of prices as costs. It might be useful to explain this distinction to help you, the reader, to better understand what is going on. From the perspective of production, costs are the moneys paid for those goods used to create a product, while the price is the money received for one such product. If the manufacturers of a product can get higher profits through the higher prices of inflation, they will then bid up the prices of those goods used to create it. These new costs are, in effect, back-fill from the higher prices for the product. Nothing has become scarcer. Nothing has become more difficult to make. Nothing which we would intrinsically consider cost has increased. Instead of an unanswerable bill we must pay, that being what we mean by saying that our costs are so much and sighing resignedly, we have another inflated price. Indeed, this inflated price for a good, being a factor in its manufacture, will come down when the inflated price of the end-product comes down. Conventional wisdom would have us run ourselves against the brick wall of high cost, high housing costs and high health care costs especially, when the real issue is whether the prices are fair or inflated.

In a market economy, the trades between buyer and seller are made freely and are thus considered fair if the buyer himself pays all of the agreed upon price for the item being traded and the seller himself receives all of the agreed upon price for the item. The usual point of unfairness brought up here is that of the seller not getting his full price due to taxes, but the more relevant point of unfairness for our purposes is that of the buyer being subsidized in his purchase. If the buyer is subsidized then the seller will not complain, of course, but the prospective buyers who were outbid can and should cry foul. The seller turned up his nose at their hard-earned, blood-sweat-and-tear-stained cash while obscenely grovelling at the promissory notes stuffed in the deep pockets of the buyer by his Daddy Debtbucks.

This unfairness is then multiplied by the debt inflation which ensues. In the case of the mortgage loan, due to its long-term and hence greater leveraging of present prices with future commitments, speculative bubbles are created in housing. The resulting real estate booms make living unaffordable, while the inevitable crashes amidst outstanding debt require making a living which is then unsustainable in the few cases where it is attainable. In the case of health insurance, a similar tragedy occurs. The sellers are the doctors and hospitals; the buyer is the patient with his Daddy Insurancebucks, whose deep pockets are made of premiums extorted from companies and governments, rather than a license to create money with debt; and those hapless and outbid prospective buyers are those patients who, honest or poor or both, have refused or been unable to participate in that scam and who are now scorned, mocked and blamed for the high medical prices caused by health insurance.[1] When the people, even those who benefit from the largesse of banks and insurers, turn around and look, they see a crushing load of debt and unpaid medical bills.

These burdens then inspire politicians to impose regulations on these and other markets which are crucial to the poor, bringing more economic power under the control of remote governments, corporations and unions

---

[1] My father, Harry Klapper, Jr., recognized health insurance for the scam it is when, having just had it foisted upon him as a federal worker, he noticed that the immediate effect of it paying for four-fifths of the bill for my regular heart-murmur checkup was to increase the stated fee fivefold, so that he paid exactly the same amount out of pocket after insurance as he did before.

by adding more rules to the process of exchange. The financing of these governmental operations, as well as the bailouts, the write-offs and the so-called *costs* created by loans and insurance, then cedes control to even more remote governments by borrowing through bonds issued in the world markets, making foreign governments and global corporations the creditors.

Of course, the aims *appear* to be laudable. By helping the poor, they would establish the authority of our power system through decency. However, the price is both exorbitant and unreasonable, because there is a simple, direct and sensible way of paying the costs of authority without simultaneously increasing the costs of operation and laying the system open to abuse. This approach is readily apparent when we stop our mindless allegiance to the well-sounding nonsense of demagogic parties. Certainly, it would not hurt for us to start listening to dispassionate reason in this and other matters of our public discourse.

The costs of authority are an obligation of all those who benefit from the system, not just those who hire the poor. These costs are not something which change from job to job, instead depending on health and other factors originating outside of the workplace. Of a truth, we all pay them. The rich may not notice it, but this is because their income from investments easily pays their survival costs. Thus, the bias of our current system is to lose money until one achieves independent wealth, that is, until one's income in the absence of work exceeds that necessary to live, this varying with the modesty of one's lifestyle.

Fortunately, there is also a legacy from which we all benefit, but which none of us still living helped to build. The work of the past, in the design of cities, towns, villages, hamlets and farms, in the buildings, streets, subways, railroads and tunnels, in the shops, stores and factories of long-standing, in the hospitals, schools and churches, in the parks, theaters and concert halls, in the habits and customs of what we regularly consume, and in the academic and folk ideas handed down to us, are all of continuous benefit to the people and commercial enterprises of today. My suggestion is to make the governments at each level the trustees for a portion of this legacy and to obligate them to provide the means for survival directly, without entitlement and its conditions, and to then dismantle the current welfare, debt and insurance system, allowing this provision of the necessities to replace it and economic regulation. In this way, the poor are not obligated to work, thus protecting them from taking dangerous jobs out of desperation, nor are they forced to sell their dearest possessions or their family life for food. Instead, lack of work brings no hardship and every penny they earn benefits them. The bias of the system is shifted in favor of the poor finding an escape from poverty, increasing their wealth and power while allowing them the home life which alone gives their affluence meaning.

I will call this proposed power system and hopefully political economy, *popular capitalism*, to differentiate it from *worker capitalism*, where economic power is dependent on employment circumstances, on belonging to a union or consultant firm, and on working for a particular company at a particular work site. It is also differentiated from what is more accurately called *crony capitalism*, where economic power is expanded through personal connections among any or all of those holding executive positions in the publicly traded companies and defended through their personal and corporate political influence, more often than not as a result of the embezzlement of the stockholder's money in order to bribe the major political parties.

I am not, however, differentiating it from *free market capitalism*, but instead asserting it to be a more honest and forthright implementation of that somewhat ambiguous notion than forms of capitalism which claim to implement it. The freedom of the market participants is only assured when their power does not depend on the sufferance of remote, widely-scoped organizations, either economic or political. Such dependence serves only to enhance the power for those organizations. With its primary goal of enhancing the power of individuals through the provision of the necessities to everyone, *popular capitalism* forthrightly assures the freedom of market participants which is essential to any true implementation of *free market capitalism*.

I would not be surprised if such power increased the efficiency of workers by giving them full freedom to choose the jobs they do best, instead of opting for ready or steady income. Yet, instead of claiming to better *worker capitalism* in its long suit — and what *crony capitalism,* under cover of its appropriation of the good name of *free market capitalism*, alleges to be its — I will be content to merely claim the greater independence and flexibility of each individual, particularly the jacks-of-all-trades among us, and to recall how company and industry towns collapse around their solitary business despite the best efforts of owners and trade unions.

I am starting, though, only with an intent. I must now show that the provision of necessities, the basis of Popular Capitalism, is possible and sustainable. To do this, I must first describe what I mean by that provision.

The Provision

The Provision

The aim of the provision of the necessities is to assure survival to everyone who abides by the rules of the power system. The manner of provision should also allow one to increase income and wealth without losing any of its benefits. Failure to do this has been the cause of the welfare trap in earlier systems and creates irrational distortions in the market. Instead, the provision should allow people to escape from poverty into financial independence with the same exertion and talent as it takes for a rich man to increase his wealth by a similar amount. That is, financial status, of itself, should not affect the ability to gain wealth. Otherwise, the market will not be able to efficiently adjust to changes in conditions, the talents and efforts of the people being misallocated on account of their current status. The provision must be universal.

This universality poses some logistical problems in its distribution for a power system holding sway over widely dispersed populations. If the cost of transport is small and the people are not too nomadic, the provision could be made by sending checks out at regular intervals: quarterly, monthly or even weekly. This would have the advantage of letting the people decide how to spend their survival allowance, avoiding government involvement in many basic industries and making changes in lifestyles easier. It would retain a bureaucracy, though mostly as database managers assuring an accurate list of addresses. The addresses could be established in conjunction with voter registration, thus sharing costs. Alternatively, bank accounts could be established for every citizen in their residence of citizenship, with the provision funds being distributed frequently, say weekly, into those accounts. With current technology, the provision can be even more efficiently distributed by electronic means. Secure access to those funds can be provided using the existing postal network, regardless of how they are distributed. Each post office would serve as a bank branch for its local citizenry, obviating the private banks.

The Provision

Despite the efficiency of the distribution, we should not fool ourselves about the cost of the provision to the government. The initial price level will cause that cost to be massive, at first. Lower domestic labor costs encouraged by such a plan would, however, soon depress prices and that cost. Also, by basing the labor market on the true cost and benefits of labor, rather than corrupting its workings with having to account for a cost of survival more properly borne by government, we will be increasing the efficiency of that market, as well as the productivity of the people. These benefits would be more massive than the cost of the program because they have as their basis the removal of the *de facto* tax on business and labor which that cost represents. These benefits are augmented by the savings from eliminating the entitlement programs, both by reducing spending and by eliminating incentives to be unproductive or to waste effort in appearing so. Still, the benefits are mostly found outside of government while the costs are mostly found within it.

Ultimately, though, even the costs which government must bear require product from the political economy as a whole. It is one thing to say that a government must pay for the provision and another to say whether they will find anyone to sell it to them. For that, we need to see whether the gross national product, or GNP[1], will be sufficient in quantity and kind to produce the provision.

As to the kind of product, we should expect that the provision would be biased towards those products that are key to survival. To the degree that non-durable demand, in the form of food and clothing, is inadequately represented currently, to that same degree, a provision would require a shift in the GNP towards those non-durables. On the other hand, if demand for housing, a durable good, is inadequately represented in the current market, then a provision would require a shift in the GNP in that direction. On balance, we may

---

1 At the time of the first edition (1986), the GNP was the primary measure of an economy's production and, therefore, of what it is capable. Since then, a subtly different measure, GDP, has been the primary measure of this economic activity and, although it is slightly more locally directed and thus more in keeping with the perspective shown here, there will, in all likelihood, be later measures of this kind that will, in turn, supplant the GDP. It is also likely that they will bear the same deficiency of an overly broad and superficial scope, not looking at the distribution of production amongst its provinces. So, rather than chase after the measure *du jour*, we will retain the use of GNP throughout.

find that any shift in the kinds of products required for the provision is within the durable and non-durable categories towards more essential products in each.

Quantity is another matter. For prosperous economies, we can expect that they are more than adequately equipped to supply the goods for a full provision. Other economies, though, may be equally well equipped, albeit at lower standards of living, for the simple reason that, many times, they do supply those goods. For those more desperate economies facing endemic famine, there are often other disasters which brought them to this pass which need to be separately addressed. However, even in the face of war and turmoil, of calamities of Nature and Man, an effort to provide the provision, although partially and supplemented with trade or aid, will bring the political economy and its people benefits that are well nigh impossible without it.

For a prosperous economy as well, if the full provision is still too frightening, a partial provision could be instituted as a compromise, until the heads of its government are convinced. We will see that it really is not that scary when we discuss its funding. For now, observe that the provision retains the whole structure of the market and makes it more efficient. Note also that the only incentive being removed is that of encouraging inefficient survival-employment; the people will still want goods and services beyond those strictly necessary for their survival and will thus retain an incentive to earn money beyond the provision to pay for them. Indeed, the only danger of the provision removing an incentive to useful work comes through attempts to pay for it by traditional but misguided means. Moreover, that misguided funding is one reason why the cost of the provision to these political economies is negligible. Most of that cost has been borne already by taxpayers paying for the tax breaks of others, by consumers paying for wages geared to the cost-of-living rather than the value of work, by charity, by welfare and, in some cases, by the victims of crime. What remains would a new contribution to the standard of living of our poor, an investment in their future productiveness, and a bolstering of the basic industries which feed, shelter and clothe them. This is the case for any form the provision might take.

The Provision

Several countries do not have the luxury of tolerable mail delivery or a population of homebodies. Some might make do by distributing the money through local offices or banks, allowing routine to take the place of delivery. Yet even this requires that the officials or tellers know who they are giving the money to. It might be impossible or too costly to establish such an apparatus. In this case, a more direct method of provision, would be in order. Such a method may even be preferred by those who could afford the first method.

This provision should, first of all, be available to the poor. Thus, the distance from their present home to where it is provided should not be so great that too much of their day is spent on receiving it. Both to reduce costs and to encourage more economical living, particularly avoiding requiring the poor to purchase automobiles or otherwise incur high transportation costs to places of employment, the provision should be provided compactly, in cities rather than sprawl. Higher rents in larger cities would be discouraged by a move to smaller pedestrian cities, where the poor may receive the provision at the same low transportation costs as in

Popular Capitalism

the metropolis: the negligible costs of walking or using the same conveyance by which, at sunk cost, one moves about the house or calls on the neighbors next door.

In considering the provision of shelter, note that since the aim is financial independence, we are not interested in developing home ownership. As currently contrived, the burdens of home ownership, or *owership* as it should more rightfully be called, are far too onerous for any poor family to also achieve financial independence; the former goal precludes the latter, though the latter, once achieved, makes the former easier to achieve. The shelter the government would provide, if provided directly, should instead be of a type which allows the people to live inexpensively and to easily earn the comforts of home for their family. It would resemble a hotel mostly for extended families of a realistic and sustainable size, so as to prevent, as is currently the case in our motorist-consumer housing, their being fractured into isolated family fragments, each having to purchase, maintain and operate their own cooking, cleaning and recreation facilities.

This may take the form of a suite composed of a

The Provision

public area with a postal bank[1], an office, a shop and a studio in which a family could conduct their business, common private areas where a family could relax and amuse themselves, sixteen private, modestly furnished double bedrooms, each with a bath, and two larger rooms with three bunk beds and three bathrooms each, for the children. A smaller number of single rooms may be provided for unattached individuals, but detachment would be discouraged as a lifestyle by making sure there are enough suites for all of the extended families and keeping the lonely rooms for loners in short supply. Lounges and hallways on the same floor as the suites would provide additional living space and recreational facilities of a somewhat less private, more public nature. These would favor use and mingling by nearby families which promotes the building of community in that neighborhood in the same way that a hallways and lounges promote the neighborhood of a college dormitory and its floors. The ground floor would have a dining hall[2] where a balanced and diverse diet of meals

---

1 See [HICKS.J.D.] for post office banks, particularly the Omaha Platform.
2 [BELLAMY] had private dining rooms that families would rent out, appealing to the rising tide of individualism in his day.

would be served, and an auditorium for public lectures and performances, both accessible from the street. All other services which a community requires, such as laundry and medical services, would be available to all residents of the hotel as part of their residency, as well as to members of the general public visiting the hotel. Thus, not only will an adequate and healthy life be had free of charge, but incrementally as well.

For example, one could move to a private house and still dine at the hotel and make use of its services. It is of course essential that there be plenty of room in these hotels, even vacancies, so that the poor are not left waiting for a room. At worst, would-be tenants could be directed to other cities, but this should happen only rarely. The only reasons for not staying in one of these hotels should be the opportunity to join a similar, but less transient community or a preference for luxury in one's personal appointments, separate from what could and would be shared in a family or community. A later chapter will discuss the former reason; the latter reason, though it should be discouraged, can nonetheless be accommodated more easily under this arrangement than under the present one.

Expenses can be kept in line by remembering what are modern luxuries. For instance, televisions are expendable; in fact, given their destructive effect on character and community, they should probably not be provided even if they were affordable. Instead, newspapers and other periodicals could be shared in the reading rooms and residents can give lectures, hold services, and put on concerts, dances and plays. Beyond being inexpensive, these are a sufficient and preferable means for a community to understand and contribute to the larger world outside its walls, without propaganda or manipulation by powers controlling that larger world.

The use of utilities can also be limited. The amounts of heating and cooling could be fixed, maybe provided to the rooms only at certain times of the day, relying on the ambient heating and cooling within a shared building for moderating temperatures. Artificial electric lighting is, arguably, a luxury, there being much to be said for living by the natural clock, but may not be that costly to provide. The use of electricity in the suites should be limited to amounts paid for by the tenants.

Use of other services, beyond a reasonable minimum, could also be provided for a fee sufficient to pay any additional labor which this may require.

The buildings for these public accommodations should be clean, free of vermin, disease and dangerous decay. Maintenance should be readily available and well supplied. High standards in plentiful public housing will then obviate most regulations of private housing. The pertinent regulations would be — as they always should be — those directing the work of public servants.

There is much room for adjustment in this description, which is only intended to give an idea of what might be directly provided and what might not. Whatever is decided is unlikely to please everybody, but that is not the aim of the provision. Rather, the goal is to provide a place to live, eat and rest and from which to go do the work one feels called to do, by the Spirit or by the commercial urgings of the people. If that work is also sufficiently remunerative, and they are not satisfied with their living conditions, they can secure a residence more to their liking. The point is that the provision frees the people to make their own choices about those things which matter most to them, chiefly their vocation and the well-being of their family.

Contrast this with the intent of the United States tax code, which forces people into the private home market, chains them to a great debt and hence handicaps them in the job market, their needing some way to pay the almighty mortgage. The poor, less able to take advantage of tax deductions, are left to less than helpful landlords of less than healthful apartment buildings. The market can adjust to losing much of its demand for housing, if that is a consequence. People are less able to deal with the present circumstances. Besides, the building trades will not immediately lose out; the building or renovation required to establish and maintain these public hotels, and structures for similar communities, will employ them handsomely.

As with housing, the meals need not be to everybody's liking. The most serious objections to certain meals, for example on religious or health grounds, can be avoided by providing some choices in the menu. This will pose no great difficulty if demand for the alternative meals is sufficient. The provision of food can also be done in cash value, separately from whatever form the provision of shelter takes.

Much will be saved in a direct provision, compared to welfare, by eliminating the bureaucratic costs of determining who is entitled to the benefits and by the administration of the benefits, which includes check-sending. Only the cost of growing, preparing and serving the food, which existed already, would remain. Further, this would shift employment from white-collar bureaucrats to blue-collar food service workers. Only some restaurants may be hurt but the work will have shifted to the public dining halls. Besides, all businesses would benefit from what, compared to present circumstances, is a subsidy of their wage costs. Of course, it is just the removal of a tax on labor formerly passed along to, then by business.

The purchase of food, whether by a government or by the people themselves using their provision cash, will be a great boon to the farmers, insofar as many families could not otherwise afford the quantity and quality of food which would now be purchased by them or on their behalf. Further, non-farm wages would be depressed by the provision, since it replaces a portion of the former wages. Hence, the price of things farmers buy will fall relative to their income. Even in the first form of provision, the demand for food, as well as adequate housing and other essential items, will increase relative to non-essentials since purchasing power will shift in favor of the poor, for whom the essentials form a greater share of their budget. Indeed, the provision, of whatever form, assures that demand for food will not fall below that needed to adequately feed the people. If the farmer can not make it under these circumstances, he will never make it. Yet if he fails, there will always be the provision to sustain him as he seeks a new career in more suitable work. He really has nothing to fear, and probably much to gain. Perhaps, then, we can eliminate the destructive and ludicrous policies which inhibit production, destroy crops and make dubious foreign policy for the sake of farmers' incomes.

The same might be said for the other troubled industries. It is time we stopped paying people to waste talents and resources, just because this is how they make their living. With the provision taking care of this, we should no longer burden productive citizens, who are willing to do what others want, with supporting selfish workers who will only do one thing and arrogantly expect to be well paid for their useless work.

The public clinic or hospital could be staffed by government-certified and possibly government-trained doctors and nurses. This would circumvent the overly restrictive policies of medical unions and professional organizations. By providing medical service directly, most of the abuses of the present United States system can be avoided. There will be no paper entitlement or insurance jungle in which to play safari. The costs of administration will be largely eliminated, as with food. Indeed, health insurance has added a windfall and thus an escalation in medical prices which direct provision can retract, resulting in further savings.

In comparing this direct form of the provision with the first, note that while some inefficiencies are introduced for those wishing to improve their lifestyle, by the same token, when the lifestyles are improved and the provision no longer accepted by some, the cost to government decreases. Also, the costs of check-sending are saved. Each approach has its advantages and disadvantages which will weigh differently in the eyes of different people or the same people in different circumstances. Moreover, the level of government delivering the services is a consideration for larger, federal republics. We should therefore leave it to each country and its people through its lowest and most immediate level of government to decide which approach to take, maybe creating some new approach.

Whatever the method, though, there will be a need to fund government in a more sensible way. Even without the provision, there is this need. Thus, as either part of Popular Capitalism or a separate suggestion, I offer my thoughts on funding the provision. Note that this approach to funding will then indicate the style of provision with which it is most consistent.

Indeed, I will offer my own preferred form of funding the provision in the chapter on popular capital. It is not offered here because it relies on further exposition, both before and within that chapter. It also will induce significant changes for all but the most *primitive* communities and is therefore not something which current statecraft will readily endorse. We should note, before proceeding, how we can gradually replace both entitlements and minimum hourly wage laws with the provision, thereby lessening the fiscal impact and disruption to those benefiting from current programs.

The first step is to end restrictions on peaceful immigration and implement the following uniform rule of naturalization: by residing a statutorily set number of weeks in a locality after one is registered for primary residence within that locality, one is eligible to become a citizen of that locality and of every federal state which includes that locality. In the United States, such an act would return its code to its Constitutional mandate. For purposes of legal equality, central to Populism, it allows registered residents at the beginning of the transition to be treated uniformly, regardless of citizenship status, and to allow children and immigrants to follow this same course in receiving the provision as they are born or immigrate to a country. I would suggest the number of weeks be set to 365, or seven years.

The Provision

The second step is to establish the increment in the weekly payment until it reaches the full provision of the necessities which, for the United States of America in our present day and circumstances, I would initially set at four dollars, so that the full weekly provision would be $1460 weekly, or roughly $76,000 annually. This may seem excessive until we realize the present burden of debt for most United States citizens is similarly excessive. It would take the average American more than a month to pay off their debt if they devoted their entire provision to that purpose. Of course, they would not be able to do that if they were unemployed with their provision as their sole source of income, or if there were children or recent immigrants in the family not receiving a full provision. Taking into account those considerations, a provision of this size would make debt retirement of a household doable over the course of a year but by no means easy during a depression, if that is of any significance for a post-debt economy.

The third step would be to establish that, going forward, the full weekly provision (FWP) should be set annually at the sum of the best estimates of the median and mean weekly cost of living per person. This would assure that the full provision is both somewhat more than most people need and somewhat more than people need on average. If the appropriate statistics are not currently available, the initial FWP amount of $1460 can be used until they are. Given the significant shifts which the provision is likely to produce in the economy, a stable FWP amount would be warranted while markets reach a new equilibrium. The statistics would also be more stable at that point and thus more reliable in setting a reasonable FWP for the following year.

The final step is to use the FWP to move from the old programs to the provision. The difference between the FWP and the actual weekly provision (AWP) would be the weekly provision shortfall (WPS). The amount received by or on behalf of an individual for entitlements in a week, or their individual weekly entitlement (IWE), would then be capped at their WPS, thus saving the government the portion of the IWE which exceeds the WPS. Thus the provision would be replacing the amounts spent on entitlement recipients.

The Provision

When the WPS reaches zero, the entitlement programs can then be safely eliminated.

A similar transition can be implemented for phasing out the minimum hourly wage. Using the rule of thumb of nuclear families averaging 2.1 children in the United States and favoring a single-wage-earner, two-parent model for that family for purposes of setting the minimum wages, we then determine the number of hours needed to support each member of that family on an average work-week of, say, 41 hours to be 10 hours. The target minimum hourly wage (TMHW) would then be the WPS divided by ten. By capping the current minimum hourly wage (CMHW) at the TMHW, each employer of general labor could save the difference between the CMHW and the TMHW for each man-hour subject to minimum wage. On the other hand, increases in the AWP will leave fewer people willing to work at the TMHW, especially as it declines. When the WPS reaches zero, the TMHW also reaches zero along with any but volunteers working at that wage. The minimum wage will then have no bearing on setting actual wages and can be eliminated due to that irrelevance.

Along the way of this transition, though, both government and industry have been able to offset much of the expense of the provision. To the reduction in wages for some minimum wage jobs we can also add the slashing of salaries for jobs which are easy, fun or pure power trips, at least where market forces are given a say. The market in any hard, grim or servile jobs for which the provision has allowed an increase in wages, will experience a moderation in that increase through certification, automation or autonomy in the workplace, all of which are made more likely in an economy where the people do not need the wages from jobs just to live. The greater efficiency and lesser waste in employment will then help to reduce costs in the general economy, further offsetting the expense of the provision. Thus, funding that provision, while not superfluous, is far less challenging than one might suppose at first sight.

The Funding

The Funding

To a generation already submerged in debt, a program of providing the necessities may seem an impossible extravagance. Even acknowledging that such a provision replaces current welfare expenses and removes almost all of the administrative costs, the scope of the program might seem too large to fund. The current approach already exceeds the capacity of our traditional revenue system. How will the new system manage the debt?

In fact, the new system will not manage any debt. Its first goal will be to eliminate the national debt. It will use taxation only sparingly; and when that is no longer necessary, it will abolish taxation and reap the savings in administrative costs from the dismantlement of the internal revenue system. The balance in revenue will be gained by using a method which has fallen into ill-repute: printing currency.

The tarnished reputation of that method is, I believe, undeserved. It has come not from its use, but from its abuse. It has been used not as a first resort, but as a last, and so has become associated with all the ills of desperate times. If we waited until a panic to tax, and then at ridiculous rates, we would shudder every time we heard of taxation. It is telling that we shudder when we hear of taxation in benign and pleasant times.

Moreover, most of the public is sadly misinformed about money, blaming printed currency for the sins of the broader money supply. Part of this comes from the curious system of money categorization used by central banks. If we are, following J. R. Hicks, to consider money as another good[1], then we ought to measure the supply of money as we measure the supply of other goods. That is, we should look at how much money is created, how much is available for re-sale and how much is consumed or destroyed. Yet the current categories of money supply count money based on

---
1 [HICKS.J.R.] pp. 58-59

where it happens to be at the time. This is like counting the supply of light bulbs by which room they are in.

A more instructive way of measuring the money supply would thus start with money creation. Creating money is a sovereign power, albeit largely abdicated here in the United States, so we start with fiscal money. For though the method of paying the expenses of government directly with a pure fiat paper currency is not now employed in this country, the necessity of paying those expenses remains. When they are paid, however they are paid, money is put into circulation by the government, that is, money is created. Conversely, when government receives revenue, however it is received, money is taken out of circulation, in other words, money is destroyed. Thus, a government deficit increases the fiscal money supply, while a government surplus decreases it.

What then of our current method of paying for deficits with newly issued debt? Does not that avoid adding to the money supply by taking in income from the sale of the bonds? No. The increase in the fiscal money supply is only delayed, not foregone. In fact, because of the necessary inducement of interest, each new bond increases the money supply more than paying directly with a pure fiat currency would. If the increase in the money supply is then realized by the issuance of pure fiat currency, because the debt is too large to be paid back with revenue, the debt advocates will immediately blame *printing money* for any inflation which may come. This is, of course, a sleight of hand to shift the blame away from government debt, the true culprit of hyperinflation. A similar misdirection is performed by government debt when it helps to create what is now the main supply of money: debt money issued by private moneylenders.

Debt money, or ledger money, is money created by banks when they makes loans. Because bank failure and financial collapse is associated with this practice, laws have been written to indirectly limit debt money creation by requiring each bank to keep a proportion of their ledger deposits in reserve. Some of the reserves are in the form of cash held in the bank's vault but, since most of the money deposited is debt money, most of the reserves have to be in some form which could be purchased with such ephemeral money. This is where the reserve assets come in. The banks use some of their deposits to buy reserve assets through the central banks, the Federal Reserve in the case of the United States. Previously, reserve assets might have been a quantity of a precious metal, such as gold. In the United States, however, we use government bonds of different terms and names, called *Treasuries* as a group, as our main reserve asset. The more federal debt we have, the more *Treasuries* are available for use as a reserve asset and, therefore, the more debt money that can be created and that can appear in depositors' ledger balances.

We have some idea of the creation of debt money and its possible limitations, so we next move on to how debt money is destroyed. This has been a puzzle to a great number of people, but we can best understand the destruction of debt money from a full understanding of its creation. A bank loan is issued by a bank from its funds, which are deposited or invested in it, to increase the borrower's balance. This loan then becomes money because the borrower's balance is recognized as money, by virtue of the bank being part of the banking system, so its increase by the bank is new money. This money is then distributed by the borrower when, immediately in most cases, they spend their increased balance, but it is not destroyed. The borrower's payments, as well as any sale of the loan contract, give the lending bank an equivalent value of the loan in existing money, so they do not destroy any debt money the loan created. Indeed, as part of the bank's reserves, loan payments increase its ability to create more debt money. Nor does a default by itself destroy the debt money, for it only prevents further transfers of existing money from the borrower to the current holder of the loan. It is not to the payment or lack of payment that we should look, but at the internal accounts of the bank, even if those accounts are not explicitly kept by the bank.

A bank's own activity can be separated into two accounts: a deposit account, similar to other depositors' accounts, and a loan account. The loan account never holds a positive balance but rather is a negative balance representing the unpaid principal on the various loans it has made. When a loan is made, and thus debt money created, an equivalent amount is deducted from the loan account balance so that the total balance over all accounts remains the same. At the same time, the debt money is converted into general money; we do not care how it is distributed afterward. The money supply has been increased by the loan amount while the bank's loan account holds the equivalent *anti-money*.

What happens then with a loan payment is that the general money received by the bank is divided into an interest portion and a principal portion. The interest portion goes into the bank's deposit account as general money, while the principal portion is converted into debt money and then is consumed by the same amount of *anti-money* in the bank's loan account. Another way to think of this is that the bank is repaying what it has borrowed from the deposit accounts, including its own. Similarly, when the loan is sold to a third party, the sale proceeds (supplemented, in the case of a sale at loss, by funds from the bank's deposit account) are divided by the bank into interest and principal, the principal being converted into debt money and then fully consuming the corresponding *anti-money* for the loan in the loan account. On the other hand, if the loan is transferred to another bank, then this operation is preceded by the new lending bank borrowing from its depositors the amount needed to purchase the loan from the original lender.

Taking this a step further, we see that a default, write-down or write-off of a loan will consist of a bank withdrawing money out of its deposit account to consume a portion or all of the remaining principal in its loan account. When a bank does not hold a sufficient balance in its deposit account to do this and cannot stall until it does, it can, in the proverbial phrase, *beg, borrow or steal* the requisite funds. In more modern terminology, the bank can get a bailout, increase its inter-bank borrowing or assess new and spurious charges and *service fees*. In some cases, banks literally steal from the depositors and, in a bank failure, this is reflected in the loss of those depositors' savings. If these accounts are insured by the government, fiscal money is being created to compensate the depositors for their share in the destruction of the debt money. So-called "credit cards" and other high risk loans come with an interest premium which anticipate the possible future loss of principal with high interest charges which lenders can accumulate prior to a likely default. In all of these cases the size of a loan account's negative balance is not reduced until a default approaches or occurs. Here, too, debt money and loan accounts are two sides of a coin.

By way of example, let us suppose that the latest fad of the public schools is for the children to construct models of various architectural works with Ice-Pop sticks and that the banks have taken to financing these projects by offering Ice-Pop Stick Loans to parents in a desperate quest for packages sufficient to allow their children to get a good grade in their Chartres project so that they can go on to a good college, then get a good job with a good salary and not be bounced from job to job as the parents were.

Let us say that the bidding up of the price of Ice-Pop Stick packages has resulted in them now being at one hundred dollars and that Mr. Smith has taken out a loan of that amount. When Mr. Smith buys the package of Ice-Pop Sticks for his daughter, Susie, the new $100 goes to the store selling the packages and Mr. Smith has a corresponding obligation to pay $100. As Mr. Smith pays down his loan with existing money from Susie's lemonade stand, which was just deposited in his account for "safe-keeping", the interest and late fees have no effect on that obligation and simply constitute a transfer of existing money from his account to the bank's deposit account. Say that he has already paid $75, of which only $60 constituted principal. Then $15 was transferred from him to the bank, with no change in the money supply. The principal amount discharged $60 of the loan obligation, which is to say, reduced the loan account of the bank by $60. The $60 consumed in this way was part of the money supply before the payments and has now been destroyed, reducing the money supply by $60. The remaining principal in the loan obligation corresponds to the $40 of new money not yet destroyed.

Since these are all internal, hypothetical accounts we are talking about, they may not be reflected in the bank's explicit bookkeeping. Thus, the aggregate listing of balances given by the banks may not give an accurate accounting from which to calculate the debt money supply. Fortunately, the negative of the balance of the possibly hypothetical loan account is easily counted by adding the principal outstanding on all active loans at each bank. Aggregating these balances gives the negative of the total debt money supply. Therefore, the total debt money supply is equal in magnitude to the total outstanding principal of all active loans in the banking system. When that principal increases, the debt money supply expands and when it decreases the debt money supply contracts. Note that the determination of the total amount of debt money supply creation and the total amount of debt money destruction ends up being an unnecessary complication when measuring their difference, which is the debt money supply.

For the fiscal and debt money supplies, a central bank serves merely as a conduit. In the case of the fiscal money supply, the treasury for a government keeps an account at its central bank, where revenues come in and expenses go out. The private banks also keep their reserve accounts at that same central bank, where reserve assets are bought and reserve assets sold on their behalf as general money is deposited and withdrawn. For these operations, no money is created or destroyed by the central bank.

Even the issuance of new paper currency for withdrawals out of the reserve accounts does not create money, just as the taking of old paper currency out of circulation does not destroy money. Paper currency used in this way is simply a placeholder for the reserve asset held by the central bank on behalf of the holders of that currency. That this is so can easily be seen from reserve assets themselves being placeholders for the deposit money placed into reserve.

Somewhat paradoxically, an increase in reserve-based currency would, other things being equal, tend to reduce the debt money supply. This is because an increase in that currency corresponds — as it constitutes the sale of private bank reserves to allow withdrawals in currency — to a reduction in the reserves of the private banks and therefore a reduction in the overall capacity of banks to lend. Since loan principal and therefore debt money is being regularly reduced over time, the result of this lessened capacity to counteract that reduction is a net decrease in the debt money supply. So *printing money* is deflationary in this, the principle case of its application under the Federal Reserve System.

There are other mechanisms available to a central bank to not only affect the money supply, but to actually create money of its own. In particular, money is sometimes created in advance by a central bank when it buys bonds. This ledger money is then destroyed when these bonds are sold to private banks and the central bank replaces the ledger money with the proceeds from the sale. However, the creation of ledger money for purchasing assets need not be followed by selling those assets. If the assets remain on the central bank's balance sheet, the created money is not destroyed. Since asset values may change, we do not use the current value of assets to measure the supply of money created. Rather, the balance sheet money supply is the sum of purchase prices minus the sum of any sale or redemption prices. In this respect, balance sheet money resembles a loan by the central bank to itself except that the principal may be underpaid or overpaid for any one asset, thus providing either an increase or decrease in its supply.

It should be noted that the main purpose of this

mechanism is not to change the total money supply, but to affect the interest rates through the bond market. A reduction in interest rates from bonds encourages a shift from bonds to capital investments and thus an expansion in business activity. In a secondary purpose, called *quantitative easing*, the central bank may want to shift private bank investment away from old loans and government bonds and toward new business and mortgage lending. An increase in the money supply, targeted to private banks, is ancillary to this purpose. In place of the old investments, the private banks are given new money in reserve to lend to businesses which may hire new employees or to lend to buyers of real estate which may encourage new construction and hiring in the building trades.

In summary, the total money supply consists of the fiscal, debt and balance sheet money supplies. For the United States, which has not issued its pure fiat paper currency, the United States Note, since 1971 and has removed it from circulation, the fiscal money supply consists of the value of coins, which are fiat money, and unrealized fiscal money in the form of

The Funding

government debt, adjusted up by the current year deficit or adjusted down by a surplus. The debt money supply consists of the aggregate outstanding principal of active bank loans. Thus, the resumption of the issuance of United States Notes, being innocent of the massive increases in the debt and thus the latent money supply from that debt, as well as being innocent of the creation of private moneylenders' debt money and of the Federal Reserve's balance sheet money, would not be the cause of inflation now or of hyperinflation in the past. Rather, the issuance of pure fiat currency and its use to pay down the federal debt actuates into the present day both the fiscal money supply and inflation of past deficits which has been stored in that debt.

Nonetheless, this unreasoned calumny against printing money persists and, associated with that bad reputation, is the hysterical fear of inflation which has been prevalent. Inflation has been called *the cruelest tax* because people on fixed incomes are hurt the most. Yet this only shows that fixed incomes are cruel, given that even a casual movement of prices will hurt people who rely on them. Since price movement is an integral part of our economic system, indeed of all adaptive economic systems, it is absurd to expect the same sense of value from a fixed income, unless it is *fixed* to a good measure of the cost of living, which is to say, not fixed at all. Those who think that a fixed bundle of goods is sufficient to the task should examine feudal contracts and figure the current value of rent paid with a few chickens and a some firewood.

The provision avoids this problem altogether, as well as the problems caused by paying for the old age pensions which are the root of our inflation concerns. These pensions, be they for the state worker or as a *social security* for the elderly, consist of taking money from people in the full vigor of life, when they can best use it to realize their dreams, and giving it back to them when they are too dead to use it. Under popular capitalism, since the necessities are provided at all ages, the young can better attain an independent and comfortable wealth, while the elderly need no longer rely on another income, fixed or otherwise, for their survival. Inflation is rid of its ballyhooed awfulness.

The Funding

We should note in passing that the provision also obviates the creation of debt money, thus inflation, by the private and central banks. Any necessity, such as shelter, is already taken care of by the provision, so there is no need for anyone to take out a mortgage loan or any other kind of loan to acquire it. Moreover, mortgages create a targeted inflation in housing which then creates its own demand. Bidders on houses with loan money behind them bid up the price, thus winning the bidding on the houses. As more house bidders use this unfair advantage — over those with only their own hard-earned cash at their disposal — housing prices are inflated to the extent that any serious bidder has to use that same unfair advantage. In the quest to put a roof over one's head, the cost of literally mortgaging one's future, of handing over to a mortgage lender the lion's share of one's prospective income, does not come into the decision of a prospective buyer to bid on a house. Indeed, these would-be residents feed into the mortgage lending game by arguing for the largest debt that will win the bidding war, enhancing their *ability to pay* far beyond what they would claim for tax men or student scholarship officers.

The same process occurs for other targeted loans, such as auto loans, inflating the sale prices of targeted goods, such as the price of an automobile when it is on the lot. The often observed decline in the price of a car once it is driven off the lot is actually the loss of the inflated loan price, car loans not generally being available to buy used cars. By disparaging the used car and the used car salesman, in particular, the propaganda machines of the automobile manufacturers have been able to bifurcate the car market. Thus, the auto buyer continues to buy new cars at artificially inflated prices from dealers who, from this price gouging alone, are far more dishonest than even their dishonest stereotype of used-car salesmen. Yet, once again, the plain fact that these new car loans pilfer the wages and the livelihood of the worker, seen in the many visits of repossession agents, does not shave one penny off of the loan-inflated price.

The use of loans for college education is a particularly wrenching application of this process. Estimates of future income are grossly exaggerated on behalf of the student in order to finance tuition, room, board and additional fees which have been inflated by loans made to students from prior years. Yet, the family itself has already demonstrated their incapacity to pay these prices in order to be eligible for the student aid of which the loans are a part. For children of college-educated parents, there is no reason to expect that they will have greater financial success and, hence, no expectation of any greater capacity of paying. Still, student loans continue to inflate college prices, since only the granting of the loan is required for that effect and not any subsequent repayment.

As yet another example, the revolving loans of so-called *credit cards*[1] inflate the prices of advertised consumer goods, which do not benefit local businesses or the wages of the local consumer since such goods are manufactured by national and international companies and sold at national and international retail store chains. With local income and spending so separated by this inducement to buy outside the local community, prices

---

[1] This is a cruel abuse of the terminology in [BELLAMY], where citizens are issued a regular credit, duly noted on their *credit cards*, from which their purchases are deducted, implementing the provision of the necessities. The modern usurper of that term should be more properly called the *debt card*.

of these national and international products become to be seen as an integral part of the *cost of living*, thus justifying the use of *the card* for any or all purchases.

Even business loans create a targeted inflation in the products businesses buy, such as advertising and machinery, which inflated prices are seen as the *cost of doing business*. With the absence of a local stock market — a Main Street stock market, not the charade on Wall — the entrepreneur is left with a choice of foregoing the usual tools of business success, and borrowing what should have been an investment. Somehow, the business borrowers convince themselves that they are superior to their more desperate fellows who run their business off of a *credit card* when clearly they are not. Like Shaw's lady, it is already established what sort of business they are in and their taking out a business loan at a more modest interest rate is mere haggling over the price.

It should be obvious from the foregoing that loans are not only unnecessary, but that they have led to a wholesale perversion of markets and should therefore be banned. If we act on this and prohibit private banks from making loans, they will lose their ability to create and destroy money. Further, the central bank loses any justification for its manipulation of the money supply since the provision makes business activity less critical to the welfare of the people and the main purported cause of bank failure, widespread loan default, is obviated by there not being any loans to default. This will leave the money supply where it should always have been: with the elected governments of the people. If the people, through their representatives, decide that government expenses should exceed revenue, they will have inflation; if they decide that revenue should exceed expenses, they will have deflation. If they decide not to use explicit taxes to raise revenue and this results in a deficit, then inflation will be their implicit tax.

Beneath its dreaded and discredited disrepute, we can then see the simple fairness of inflation as a tax. No accountant or lawyer can avoid it. The only loophole is the purchase of goods which retain their value. Yet with the bare needs supplied, a poor worker can invest as great a share of his further income in such goods as his wealthy neighbor. The ones who can't use this loophole are those who spend the money they earn on the more fleeting pleasures of life, as is their choice, and which, incidentally, spurs the current economy.

Its main defect is a defect it shares with taxation: it has a permanent effect on the economy, but only a temporary effect on the treasury. Even here, it is better than taxation. General inflation just pushes prices up, at worst feeding on itself when expected. Taxation misallocates resources and forces the economy to work below efficient capacity, as well as diverting powerful minds to the manipulation of its code. Its brutal stupidity reveals its ancestry in plunder and extortion.

Other so-called defects of inflation are, in fact, defects in the way governments try to limit it or its effects. Through price controls, discount lending and monetary policies, through protectionism, subsidies, bailouts and collective bargaining *rights*, through insurance and pensions, governments try to protect special interests and political supporters from one parameter in a market with millions of participants. They forget that the free market is the best arbiter of our demand and, though this stern judge rudely wakens us from our free-spending, free-credit dreams, it is because reality is expensive and our happiest state is achieved through a careful reckoning of its costs.

Nonetheless, this should not make us settle on inflation as the only means of funding our system. For one thing, the value of fiat currency ultimately depends on its being returned to the government, eventually, as revenue. Further, continual inflation disrupts the market more than would otherwise be warranted. We do need a stabilizing mechanism, just not of a market-perverting kind. Toward this end, we turn first to that other bane of conventional wisdom: government investment.

People who will not bat an eye at a trillion dollar government debt will be yelling socialism or worse if government invests its rare surpluses. There is, however, a real concern behind those fears. If it were to invest in particular firms, a government could easily lose partiality. Of course, it easily loses partiality without this, but that is another story. The thing to avoid is for a government to be operating the businesses it favors at a loss and funding them with public money.

We can avoid this in a number of ways. First, the federal government's investment can be indirect, through a financial market driven by local decisions. Second, the structure of the invested businesses can be, like all large and established corporations, bureaucratic and institutionalized, and can therefore be organized and operated like a government agency, all employees — and especially the senior management — being paid on a civil service scale, thus preventing the siphoning off of profits to privilege at the expense of investors. Third, the form of the investment can be a government providing a site and access to materials, fuel, workers, and legal protection, similarly to large corporations investing in real estate for their offices and factories, with all the necessary permits and accesses attended to. With the investments being driven by the people, with management costs minimized and with no outlays of cash, such investments will be able to gain the income needed to fund government.

Another form of revenue, similar to this, is to be found in the membership dues which many towns claim in the form of property taxes. As the right to investment returns just cited is based on the site, access and legal standing of a business being recognized by government, the right to these membership dues is based on the legal recognition accorded by the town of the domain of each household within it. At the federal level, these dues could be levied on the States, rather than directly on individuals or families. The States themselves can use these same two sources of revenue to meet their expenses and pay their membership dues. In any event, the people in each State will be better able to fund their State government once their citizens have the provision of the necessities.

The domain of a government thus constitutes an endowment which will make other forms of revenue unnecessary. Both membership dues and net return on investment in the companies within their domain allows a government to recoup funds spent on the provision and other government expenses. When the economy contracts, the net loss from investment would act as a stimulus, and when it expands, the net return from investment would take money out of the economy, moderating the expansion. If necessary, the legislature can increase the dues or reduce government salaries to create a surplus with which to reduce the fiscal money supply. Because of the provision, there will be no political pressures of any consequence to discourage these actions, both after liquidating the debt and at any point thereafter where it may be warranted. This likely conclusion to large printing will help nip any inflation hysteria in the bud.

As to the financial market, it should be operated as a federal judicial bank system run by the courts. Unlike the central banking systems in other countries, none of the banks in this system will make investments or extend loans. The sole purpose of a judicial bank is to adjudicate and administer financial contracts and operate markets. The coordinating branch of this system will be the federal branch, which will have only state treasuries and the federally-scoped companies, in which the states invest, as depositors. The federal treasury will have an account for the disbursement of the provision and the receipt of the state membership dues and half of the revenue from the federally-scoped companies which, as federal agencies, are subject to the strict

The Funding

accounting of their revenue. Thus federal investment is blind and the states are given power over the federal level of the economy in this system, making it more federal than the federal reserve system it will replace.

The distribution of actual currency can be performed by offices of the market at the main headquarters of each state branch. The same federal structure is applied to each federal or quasi-federal level down to the most local. It is at the neighborhood or hamlet offices that the people would have their accounts and access to their currency. These offices might be most ably sited in local post office buildings, using postal transportation to move currency and using enhanced postal communications to perform ledger transactions securely. Indeed, the post office can serve as the transportation and communications department.[1]

It is at this point that we see the capitalist aspect of popular capitalism. For an investor in capital projects bears the risk of a lesser return on his investment with the resale value of the physical capital as the minimum

---

1   Thus combining Populist calls [HICKS.J.D.][WOODWARD] for postal banks and for government ownership of transportation and communication.

return of a failed enterprise. No capitalist investor wants to subject the bulk of his savings to the roller-coaster ride of speculation, from which he is more likely to lose than gain money, albeit with bigger gains if he wins. The entrepreneur, in creating investment opportunities, is taking the larger risks with his efforts, so that his larger returns can hardly be said to be speculative. Bringing these two together is the non-speculative mechanism of capitalism, as opposed to the entirely speculative nature of debt and a debt-based economy.

A moment's reflection will show how debt and speculation are related. As discussed earlier, when debt is offered, it creates more money chasing after the same set of goods. Whether it is general consumer debt directed at consumer goods or more restricted to a store or a product, such as housing, the set of goods is limited to some degree. Therefore, the credit creates price inflation in those goods. This begins the speculative rise as it is followed by higher pay to those selling those goods, and hence more purchasing power for them to buy other goods which then increase others pay. When this rise in prices exceeds the willingness and ability of consumers to pay, along with the servicing of their existing debt, sales decline, pay is cut, purchasing power is reduced and the speculative bubble bursts.

This same speculation is played out simultaneously in the stock market. As stock prices inflate, investors can earn handsome profits by day trading with little risk. Even longer term investors participate in the speculation by selling at a price which is not sustainable in the future. The investor buying at the speculative price is then left holding the bag when the general prices moderate and the stock prices decline. It may seem odd to the casual observer to recommend capitalism as a remedy for stock market speculation but the operation of the stock market in this case is debt-based and not capital-based.

A capital-based stock market is one where investors offer up money to allow a company to purchase machinery, capital, that will hopefully increase profits, which will then be returned to investors through dividends. If the dividends are distributed, the price of the stock will not increase as much and there is less opportunity for speculation. Moreover, if the true profits are subject to dividends, rather than being diverted to executive salaries and perquisites, stock price inflation is dampened still further. Finally, if the small investor is realizing a good return through dividends rather than by trading, they are more likely to hold onto their stock despite any changes in its trade price.

When stock is traded in such a market, its price represents the present value of the expected stream of dividends over time. Such a dull and prosaic outcome to stock investing eliminates any hope of *making a killing* in the stock market and the speculative spirit arising from such aspirations. A more sober spirit prevails in the wider world, so that the people are less likely to gamble away their hopes with lottery tickets or to be subject to the blandishments of credit card companies. This is not to say that these operations would completely disappear, but that a capital-based stock market will help to greatly curtail them.

It is also not to say that all debt should be eliminated. Commercial paper and an equivalent short-term lending to individuals is useful when receipts lag slightly behind expenses. A funds market that facilitates cash flow, without opening the door to default, was and remains the only justification for debt. The management of this market should also be a function of the judicial bank, since it is essential that such lending stay within guidelines which assure that the debt is truly short term and not defaulted.

Thus we may require that each loan be limited by a maximum term, followed by lending for at least as long a time. In a transition from the current debt system, the conversion to shorter-term debt, and its subsequent retirement, can be aided by using of a portion of each weekly provision to repay the loan on an automatic basis. A similar mechanism can be used for companies, but this awaits further discussion about companies under popular capitalism. A local market can be created in the now-short-term debts where, at the close of each business day, the daily interest rate is raised if debits exceed credits and lowered if credits exceed debits, with the interest for debits being slightly higher than that for credits. The total interest credited to positive accounts is rounded down and that debited from negative accounts is rounded up. This lets low demand for commercial paper reach equilibrium at a daily interest rate of 0% for credits and, say, 0.01% for debits. The local judicial bank's mission is to come as close as it can to clearing daily and over the longer term by a judicious setting of the interest rate. The local treasury, by depositing funds as a reserve, can allow the bank to process withdrawals and new loans when they exceed new deposits and the repayment of the debts. In this way, a small though vital cash flow is preserved, free from the terrors of bank runs or failures, as well as from the schemes of confidence men and latter-day princes.

We can now set aside the minor role of banking in handling these small debts and deal with the larger issue of capital, where the more substantial economic tasks are performed. The returns from these investments will help fund the provision and therefore help determine whether the net effect of our program is inflationary, deflationary or stable. We have sketched this out using the more familiar figures of the present day, though these may not remain past a transitional period. The discussion cannot really begin, though, before we understand how capital relates to the daily life of people living under a political economic system, specifically our proposed popular capitalism. For this, we must reach back to some ancient concepts which lie at the heart of citizenship and the household.

The Polis and the Oikos

We now need to step back to ancient themes and equally ancient disputes because we cannot truly come to an understanding of the political economy until we resolve the ancient conflict in those two words which have been played out in every age. Only then can we then understand the derived notion of capital and how it can be made to serve the interests of individual people.

Modern ears, which have been inured to the conflict in the phrase political economy by repetition, rely on the corresponding unfamiliarity of the phrase popular capital to deem it an oxymoron. Stripping away the illusion of familiarity, we see that *political economy* is no less an oxymoron and that we have been sweeping its apparent contradictions under the rug. Indeed, popular capital will resolve the conflict in that phrase and show that *political economy* need not be an oxymoron, for theirs is the same conflict.

The ancient Greeks used the words, πόλις and οἶκος, the *polis* and *oikos* in our *politics* and *economics*, to denote two distinct areas of life and forms of society. The *polis* is the life about town and the *oikos* is the life of the household. By extension, the *polis*, being rooted in markets and public forums, became associated with the organization of cities. The *oikos*, being rooted in garden and hearth, became linked with the organization of the country. Like the city mouse and country mouse of storybooks, the *polis* and the *oikos* have coexisted uneasily for centuries.

This suspicion and distrust, long festering, comes to the fore, now and then, as the *oikos* occasionally resists the constant attempts of the *polis* to take power away from it. A little reflection shows that this conflict between the urbane and the rustic, between the swaggering pretension of empire and the intimate humility of villagers, between offices and farms, between commercial development and the fallow fields and backwoods of the country, that is, in all of its sundry manifestations, the conflict between *polis* and *oikos* form the basis of much of our history.

This conflict even provided the grist for populism through various agrarian revolts. And yet this same populism shows the way to its resolution. By advocating the distribution of power to the people, individually and without exception, populism cuts to the heart of the matter and asks whether these forms of organization are directed toward assuring that every person has enough power to be free. Such questions are often ignored by those who promulgate a stereotype of the Populist which casts sinister aspersions on his call to give the little guy a leg up on the rich or powerful bullies of our world and insinuates that such speech is a demagogic cover for plunder. The source of such slander is revealed in these same stereotypes being, more accurately, the demagogic cover for control by partisan, career politicians.

The Populist does not call for the wealthy man to be dispossessed of his great wealth, but that he share some with the poor. The Populist does not engage in class warfare, but seeks to end the economic warfare against the small farmer, the local factory and the mom-and-pop store. The Populist seeks to bring each household into harmony with its neighborhood, agriculture into harmony with manufacture, the *oikos* into harmony with the *polis*. Toward that end, this Populist presents to you a capitalism which establishes that harmony. Here you will find a capitalism not based on manipulation and greed, but on the joining of households into a community. Say farewell to the crony capitalism, that thin veneer over mercantilism, with its slavery to debt, to jobs and to gold, with its influence peddling, government contracts and special favors, bailouts and deals. Welcome today a popular capitalism, a capitalism of the people, giving them power individually and without exception.

To understand this transformation from conflict into harmony, we need to delve into the treatment of *oikos* and *polis* in Aristotle's *The Politics*. There we are presented what we now call the conservative political view, in response to Plato's liberal political view. In Book I, Aristotle fabricates a history of the household whose purpose does not become apparent until we read in Book III, Chapter 1 that "what effectively distinguishes the citizen from all others is his

The Polis and the Oikos

participation in Judgment and Authority"[1]. Since Aristotle considers "menial work" an impediment to that participation, to the extent that he questions whether "free workers" can be citizens in Chapter 5, and since he views people functionally, like organs in a body, he can only have citizens if there are people who do not work. This, in turn, requires that the *oikos* consist primarily of the master who rules and women and slaves who obey and do the work. Thus, though he allows for different forms of the *polis* evolving, Aristotle keeps his *oikos* in an arrested stage of development, ignoring any other form the household might take. One wonders what form the *oikos* of a "free worker" might have taken in Athens, but one's curiosity is never sated. The only form of the *oikos* we are allowed to consider is the aristocratic one and the only way it interacts with the *polis* is through its lord and, on behalf of future *oikoi*, its lords apparent.

For that *oikos* to survive past its initial master in the form of an *oikos* for each heir, its property in land and slaves must increase to allow for a sufficient share

---

1 [ARISTOTLE] p. 102

to be handed down to the next generation, which repeats the process. So, in Book I, Chapter 4, Aristotle states that "the acquisition of property [is] part of the economics of the household"[1], before describing slaves as tools his form of *oikos* needs in order to make a living.

The American reader will protest at this point that the conservative no longer supports slavery and hasn't since the Democrats lost the Civil War. They will be in error. Both conservatives and liberals support wage slavery, where the employed are tools of interstate and international corporations, and indeed applaud increases in employment rather than financial independence. Also, in prosperous households in rural sprawl, both conservative and liberal homeowners use so-called "illegal" immigrants as *de facto* slaves, if only to maintain their lawns.

The dispute between the conservatives and liberals is not on the issue eliminating slavery in all of its manifestations, or even whether slaves should serve the Aristotelian *oikos* or the modern *polis*. Rather, their

---
[1] [ARISTOTLE] p. 31

dispute is centered on which section of the *polis* should have their slaves. The conservative would rather have slave labor for businesses and in the homes of the well-to-do, in order to spare the corporate and distinguished citizen from performing or fully paying for menial work. The liberal would rather have entitlement slaves to help get their politicians elected and justify large government bureaucracies, as well as having immigrant slaves picking weeds for government officials.

Though we can certainly go on about the folly of the liberal and conservative positions, the point which needs to be made is that the error of Aristotle which got us into this quandary of slavery and hypocrisy was his definition of citizen. This, in turn, is a consequence of another, that "the state is the sum total of its citizens". What Aristotle left out of this equation is the *oikos*, which he apparently only used as a prop for his history of the formation of the *polis* and the citizenry. Instead of including the *oikos* in his model of the *polis*, Aristotle sloughs it off and only takes one of its members as part of the *polis*. A more integrated model would define the *polis* as the sum total of its *oikoi*, where their organization is a key part of classification of the *polis* rather than made to fit the one despotic and unsustainable mold.

Of course, classification is not our concern here, but populism. Getting power to the people, individually and without exception, and keeping it there is no easy task. Some individuals may amass great power over their fellows by using their political skills to gain control over the organs of government through party positions and elective office. Other individuals may amass great power over their fellows by using their personal wealth to gain control over the economy through financial and land purchases. Fortunately, a more developed form of the *oikos* and a more sensible definition of property can prevent this from happening. The first is seen in our own American rites of passage and the second in an old Populist demand[1]. The first we will suggestively name the *college* — *as* it resembles the educational institution in permanence, nurture and security — showing how those features protect its

---

1 See [HICKS.J.D.] and [WOODWARD] for this and other demands of the Populists, set in a historical and biographical context.

residents from the political and economic ambitions of others, both within and without its walls. The second, *popular capital*, replaces both the private, renegade property in industry and institutions by corporations and the remote, renegade governments which, under the pretext of that private abuse, seek to regulate corporations by subjugating the people. In their place, *popular capital* establishes the stewardship of each industry and institution in the local *polis* by those of its *oikoi* who have chosen to assume it. Through this design, no avenue will be given for a public or a private usurper to gain control of the local *polis* or the *oikos*. This design, given in brief outline here, also suggests that the conflict between the *polis* and the *oikos* will be resolved by basing the construction of the *polis* on a stable *oikos*, to which we now turn our attention.

The College

The College

Many of us grew up in the American version of the Aristotelian household with Dad the benevolent despot, Mom the homemaker and those dependable mechanical slaves, the appliances and the lawnmower. From there, most of us who received our high school diploma then moved into a collegial household of fellow scholars. Some of us moved from that original dormitory, where we only performed a few of the chores of common living, into group houses where we at least cooked our meals and sometimes even grew our own food. After earning our degrees, we then struck out on our own, often sharing houses with other recent graduates and young professionals. For many years, we might have lived in collegial households before finally regressing to the Aristotelian household once we wed our spouse. We remember those years with some fondness and, often, they are the fondest of our college and young adult memories. Many of us questioned the forced impermanence of those households and some, especially at the universities, did their best to resist an end to a blissful communal life by becoming resident advisers or graduate students. And then, years after finally moving away, we delight in coming back as alumni and alumnae to stay in the dorm rooms, eat at the college cafeteria and attend some lectures in a nostalgic return to the communal household at our *alma mater*.

As for the Aristotelian households to which we have moved, these dissolve through divorce, death and the children growing up, with an impermanence which is not forced because they are too small and too imperious to last more than a generation. Never mind coming, you can never stay home in such households. In a kingdom, which the Aristotelian household most closely resembles, there must be a succession or an end, a death of the realm. "The King is dead" comes before "Long live the King". Returning to such a home would be a descent to the tomb.

A collegial household large enough to establish a residential inertia, yet with few enough member families to be run by consensus, is neither small nor imperious. With a few thousand people, as you would find at a small liberal arts college, without the academic imperative of leaving with your degree, and with sufficient farmland to assure your survival without working outside of the household, you *can* stay home. Moreover, that home would be no mere nursery, no nest which you must outgrow, but a more developed form of the household, of the *oikos*, designed to hold the family you left when you went off to your academic college and to make your way in the world, as if you never left, as if you never needed to leave but were always there and thus where you can be born, can blossom, mature, bear fruit and die, while the home remains indefinitely. There is no imperative to acquire more land or more money to pass on to secure the future of one's heirs. There is no need for those heirs, ensconced in their own small manor, to sell off your old manor, often as an unwelcome accompaniment to their grief.

In place of this turmoil, the collegial household offers shelter out of a revolving stock of housing to a child, before they become an heir. Then, when the time comes, they can mourn the death of their parents in peace. The personal effects are passed down and, after a decent interval, the room is occupied by other family members, maybe some children who had been crowded into one of the other rooms. Through all of this ebb and flow of life and death, the collegial household remains, itself neither purchased nor sold. Instead, it is its own legal unit of residence, of people living together under the same rules and considered by the law as a group. Since this is the sense which the word *college* gets from its Latin root, we will hereinafter use that word to refer to the collegial household.[1]

Because of this permanence, it is all the more important that the formation of a college, as well as any changes in membership, preserve the freedoms of all

---

[1] See [DAVIS] for the history of colleges and other groups which formed the legal basis of corporations. The corporate person is a vestigial claim from the communal roots of corporations.

members of age. Adult citizens should be allowed to leave colleges freely, though joining a college without invitation should be approved by unanimous consent of the current adult residents of that college. Certainly, no one should be a prisoner in their own home, as also there should be no doubt that they are welcome to stay. The only exception to this should be in the case of a depleted college membership when there are citizens without a college wanting to join that college. Then applicants for membership should be allowed to join that college up to the family causing the college to reach or surpass the minimum size.

The laws should also, in the areas properly under their control, which is to say in the provision and other publicly managed payments, encourage a greater equality of college members so that a family does not have to move from college to college in order to be fairly treated. Thus, each college family should receive an equal share in revenues from its investments and in income from shop rentals. Each adult, citizen member of a family would have a similar equality within their family, through a similar means. The curse of many agrarian societies where there is a lord ruling over his serfs or slaves is thus avoided by putting all adults on an equal footing within the college. The college then forms a society closer to a farming commune than that of a feudal manor, an antebellum Southern plantation or their modern equivalent, the sprawl home surrounded by patches of macadam and grass, neither of which its occupants can eat.

The crucial way in which the college differs from a commune, the intermediate organization of its families, also protects its members from oppressive inequity, if those families are allowed to be extended families. With a family size of about forty-two people, the extended family unit is considerably more stable and powerful than nuclear families. Grandparents and great-grandparents can remain and be cared for by their children as these grow older, some adding a spouse and children of their own, some leaving to live with their spouse's family and some remaining single or childless. Childless uncles and aunts can stay close to their nieces and nephews, at first doting on, then sharing confidences and, finally, being cared for as if they were natural parents. The extended family would typically be composed of a youngest generation of about seven boys and seven girls, a parental generation of about seven couples or roommates, and a generation of about seven pairs of grandparents or grandaunt and granduncle roommates. There may be elderly family members of the great-grandparent generation and fewer children, or some unevenness in the generations, but there is a far greater likelihood of stability in the size of an extended family if the pressures to marry and bear grandchildren can be distributed among fourteen people of marriageable and child-rearing age than if they fall squarely on the only child or a few siblings.

To accommodate this family size comfortably, an apartment could have sixteen regular-sized bedrooms for the adults or couples with infants and toddlers. For children too old for their parent's rooms, there would be a triple-sized room for the boys and a triple-sized room for the girls, each with three bunk beds. In this way, an extended family living in such an apartment can comfortably include thirty-two adults and teenagers, with plenty of room for the couples' young children, and up to six each of the older boys and girls. It is therefore expected that most extended families could reside there indefinitely without the inclination to move, much less the need to do so.

In a college of ninety-six of these very stable families and a transitional population equivalent in size to four families, the total population corresponding to a target college size of forty-two hundred persons, an individual is well protected by his family and other families in the college from any would-be cult leader, such as seem to afflict many smaller communes. No one person can be father of a college consisting almost entirely of extended families, each with many fathers spanning multiple generations, and therefore no one can presume upon such sweeping parental authority to enact their tyrannical schemes. Stability of place also works against tyranny arising from one family in a hundred since each of the other families will assert their claim to continued residence without adhering to whatever political creed is being put forward by any family for its own aggrandizement. People are more easily manipulated and controlled when their families are on the run or when they have to be mobile for their careers than when their families have lived in the same home for generations and when they are certain that they can remain there for many generations more. The cultic appeal to certainty is an offer of a stable, though metaphorical home. That appeal falls on the deaf ears of people who have the stability of a real home.

Thus people are made safe from petty tyrannies in a college, but how does a college help keep a wealthy few from dominating the other residents? First, because your housemates are your companions, rich and poor in a common bond. Second, if the premises are owned, they are owned in common; the rich kid can't threaten to take it away. Third, each resident can have their own possessions in their own room and have their own bank account, a wealth giving independence from monopoly power.[1] Fourth, the college assures that food is grown on their common land and prepared for their common sustenance, not at the sufferance of anyone with more

---

[1] See [KEFAUVER] for an account of monopoly power seeking victims in local businesses dependent on regular sales for their survival. The deep pockets of regional and interstate companies allow them to take a loss on a low price in the area served by the locals until that competition has folded from a lack of sales revenue for weeks or months. Then the prices go back up.

power or wealth. Lastly, the common dwelling provides shelter to rich and poor housemates alike.

To this defense of the individual against a wealthy fellow resident can be added the power granted by the provision of the necessities, especially when it is suitably modified to account for the role of the *oikos*. If a portion of the provision is placed into the individual's account and a portion, directly or indirectly, into that of the college, then that individual not only has the funds to individually provide for individual necessities like clothing, they also make a significant and consistent contribution to the college on which that college then relies. The individual is both desired by the college and in good standing with it. The contributions which come through the individual then allow the college to reward those members who farm the land, raise the animals, cook the food, launder the clothes and perform other tasks which provide and distribute the real necessities of the college and thereby make it self-sustaining and independent. No longer are the people held in thrall to the rich or the powerful for jobs, whose only appeal to the people is to enable them to acquire the income they need to pay for groceries and the rent. Like members of our own family, members of a college are still permitted to live when they are too sick, old or exhausted to work, too young to be safely and usefully hired, too numerous compared to overall consumer demand for their work to be worth what our bias calls a *living wage*, too aligned to the needs of a bygone time to be employed without further training, or, taking the converse case, too rich in things to have a need for wage income. Whatever their circumstance or condition, they still bring to their college, by virtue of their residency alone, direct and indirect allocations of the provision of the necessities and are therefore still valuable to the college.

This is arguably the greatest freedom of the poor from the power of the rich, as its lack has been a staple of melodrama. There is no villain evicting the poor family out of their homes in the dead of winter because they could not pay the rent or mortgage after he has stolen their money. The husband and father is not arrested for stealing a loaf of bread to support his family after he lost his job because some nephew of his boss fancied his wife. The supposed orphan does not become a slave. Those episodes do not and could not play in a world where one's home and sustenance is free from any need for a wage income. For the same reason, real life episodes of widespread famine due to the majority of the population being both landless and unemployed are also impossible with colleges and the provision.

The individual is also protected from powerful organizations when the college, as the locative basis of citizenship, is the only kind of party permitted to hold shares in local institutions. This keeps the power of those institutions within the community and away from outside interests which the wealthy could use to control them. This arrangement also mutes any undue influence from within by any one college member. The power over those institutions is directly vested in the college, which is the strength and protection of the individual.

Indeed, such institutions become extensions of the identity of each person in the shareholding colleges because the college is itself an extension of the identity of its members. Such extensions of identity are made with far greater purpose than the more contrived bases of calls for support from country, state or political party.

The collegial farming household would be more thoroughly the nourishing mother, *alma mater*, than any academic institution to which we give that name, and would therefore lay claim to our first allegiance outside of our immediate family. After our college, we next may place our allegiance with those institutions in which our college regularly invests even as the allegiance of those institutions would primarily be with those colleges who fund them each week. Such symbiotic relationships, so lacking in the *buy it and forget it* stock ownership of our current corporations, is a sure defense against alien takeovers by forces which are hostile to the local people and their individual power.

A further step toward assuring the independence and power of the individual is that the relationship between the *oikos* and the first level of the polis, which meet on the street, can be formalized by law to promote equal entrepreneurial opportunity in its street shops. Such laws could stipulate that the college may rent street shop space only to its members, with each family limited to a share in only one street shop. The rent for a street shop of similar size and design as the extended family apartments could be reasonably fixed at the same rental that members of an extended family would pay, in total, for their apartment. If their apartment account receives the same share of the provision as is paid for each room, each extended family could pay the rent of a street shop by itself, using just the provision. Therefore, a small group of poor families, using just the provision, could rent the space for a street shop, pay for street shop expenses of the same amount and still have most of their apartment funds for other expenses.

Within this structure, the rich and their families can run a street shop, but not prevent other families from running theirs. The money from the street shop rent can then be divided equally between the college and the *polis* as is appropriate to the relationship which places a shop on a street and gives access to shoppers. Beyond its share of the rent money, the *polis* would have no further share in the proceeds of the shop, leaving the shop owners free to benefit fully in their own success while not placing an undue barrier against it. Also, with no regulations or other avenues to special advantages for the wealthy, these shops provide a way for those of modest means to earn some luxuries while realizing their dreams. Note that these funds can be distributed automatically by the judicial bank without relying on the cooperation of any entity in the chain of transactions. With that resolution of required payments, each street shop is free to arrange its affairs as it sees fit, to decide by consensus how each extended family will contribute beyond any automatic contributions and how they will be rewarded for their contribution.

In all these ways, individual wealth is denied power over other individuals. Thus, beyond providing an additional protection against the power of other individuals, the *oikos* or the *polis*, a surfeit of financial wealth can only serve two ends: to fulfill one's destiny by creating new products or services, and to purchase the products and services of others' destinies. Money which is honestly earned will then be spent to make dreams come true, if only in the chance to try. Thus, money circulates to facilitate more trade as it was always meant to do.

This discussion does not duly consider the more intimate living arrangements and the important role of the nuclear family, of the couple with their young children, in the household. In our political economy, this social unit has been largely superseded in its civic role as a political and social unit by the college. What remains is its nesting role and the place it provides for the intimacy of a couple. For both purposes, physical and financial room needs to be made which is shared in common by the couple, yet preserving individuality and independence for each partner. Financially, this can better be done by allocating a portion of each partner's publicly distributed income — the sum of the provision, their share of college revenue and their wages, if any, from public employment of any kind — into a common fund for family expenses than, as is currently the case, by leaving it to the couple to come up with a no more equitable distribution after considerably more conflict and heartache. As for accommodations, besides their common space, there should be made available, as may be required for the couple's joint work or the individual work of each partner, an office, shop and studio in their family apartment, easily accessible to other members of the college wishing to purchase their products or to use their services. In addition, the operation of the family postal bank, also situated in the apartment, lets parents enjoy a less commercial interaction with their neighbors in the college, the family postal bank job being, in fact, a civil service position with wages on a civil service pay scale, paid by the judicial bank system, separately from any service fees collected. The proximity of these work locations to the room where their babies sleep, as well as the ability of workers to perform many of these jobs with their small children, would be a great comfort to new parents, especially, as they are able to resume their adult lives without the stress and isolation so prevalent in our current workplaces and residences.

In considering the extended family populating the rest of their apartment, there is less necessity for an immediate work location and more opportunity in work located in the rest of the college, in its street shops and beyond. Therefore, the office, shop, studio and postal bank provide sufficient room for the extended family to conduct their hallway enterprises. A parlor space to greet visitors to those enterprises or to the family as a whole, a formal gathering room, an informal area for entertainment and a complement of closets including full bathrooms in each private room and half-baths for each public space complete the extended family's need for rooms. The composting of human waste from these bathrooms in the basements of the college would eliminate sewage while returning nutrients to the soil. Likewise, the use of greywater draining from its tubs and sinks for hydroponics, irrigation and marshes frees the college from any need for an external sewer pipe. The college can then be self-sustaining and self-contained in its use and disposal of natural resources. This form of the *oikos* thus lives up to another of its derived words: ecosystem.

Some may feel that we missed two rooms which form the basis of the traditional home: the kitchen and the dining room. For a large, extended family these rooms are correspondingly large and the common assumption is that they are also efficient. However, daily food preparation and serving is more efficiently performed by the college as a whole, a fact clearly demonstrated by the appeal of public restaurants for even the largest extended families. Moreover, intimacy is often established in a community by potluck suppers and other common meals, while a family already shares a deeper intimacy without the family supper. For those special family occasions and celebrations, where a large family is made larger still by inviting distant cousins and assorted friends to dinner, the college dining hall provides more commodious room and seating than any private residence, even more than many banquet halls, but at the attractive rental price of free. The food can be cooked by the family hosting the event, with or without the assistance from other members of the college, in a fully equipped college kitchen. Therefore, the omission of those rooms from the family apartment floor plan avoids the absurdity and waste of each family having a dining room and kitchen which is only fully used a few days in the year.

Away from domestic architecture, the financial arrangements of couples can be applied more generally by a rule to divide the publicly distributed income of each individual into four equal portions: one with that individual, one to the room or couple account, one to the apartment or extended family account and the last to the college account. If the shop, the postal bank and each of the sixteen regular bedrooms has a rent of one-quarter of a provision, if the office and the studio, each being of double size, has a rent of a half provision, and if each of the two larger bedrooms, being of triple size, has a rent of three-quarters of a provision, then the rent for a college apartment would be seven provisions. A minimal extended family of twenty-eight members thus could pay for that rent through its share of the provision alone. As long as each of the sixteen regular bedrooms is occupied and the boys and girls rooms are fully occupied, or there is one regular bedroom with two adults for each empty bed in the bunks, there will be enough in provision payments to pay the rent. Even shy of this occupancy, the apartment's share of the provision can be used to cover a shortfall, up to a point.

When all of the rent comes out of the room accounts, the provision portion of the weekly apartment funds — seven provisions from the minimum apartment occupancy of twenty-eight — can be used for a family's share of the weekly rent and expenses of a street shop. Setting the amount allocated for weekly shop expenses to that allocated for rent, the total weekly allocation for each street shop would be fourteen provisions. If four extended families are given responsibility over each of the twenty-four street shops, the amount coming from each family for this purpose would be three-and-a-half provisions. This leaves three-and-a-half provisions or more remaining for each extended family which may be used, as the family decides, to heat their apartment, to fill their baths or run their showers, to run electrical devices, to furnish, decorate and equip their common areas, to purchase materials and equipment for their common pursuits, to maintain a common wardrobe or to add to a family library for their mutual edification and entertainment. Larger extended families would have more leeway in providing for their life together.

Considering next the accommodations for those individuals in transition, we allow the same occupancy and vacancy as in the apartments to reckon the number of bedrooms corresponding to one family. Since each of the regular bedrooms has double-occupancy and since each apartment allows for a vacancy of two for each family at its target size of forty-two persons, the number of bedrooms equivalent to a family would be half forty-four or twenty-two. Thus, eighty-eight bedrooms would be set aside in a guest house on the college grounds. The occupants of the guest house would be longtime guests who are living at the college but not with any one extended family, prospective members and those in transition from one extended family to another. Though the guest house may hold as many as one hundred and seventy-six occupants, these will not operate a street or home shop, or share in the revenue from these or from the college investments, so there is no necessity for any level of occupancy there. The occupants will, however, retain half of the provision, the apartment share being added to their own.

As for the services which we seek or which are thrust upon us by local governments or employers, such as are still necessary for the operation of the colleges, can be provided by members hired and equipped out of college funds, in a manner decided by the consensus of college families and members, or be offered by families and members in their offices and shops. Thus, though an extended family may pride itself on having, among their kin, physicians, professors, lawyers, plumbers, electricians, carpenters, potters and farmers, this need not be the case for any one family in the college. For medical emergencies, it is sufficient to have a doctor in the house. Anything beyond the capability of a college, of course, remains the concern of the *polis*, but there is no reason for a college of moderate size not to have a clinic, to hold lectures, to have one of its own represent it or file motions on its behalf, to keep the building in good working order and to replace bowls and plates.

The more developed form of the *oikos*, to summarize from the above, consists of the individual, the intimate family, the extended family and the college. The provision of the necessities through the individual assures their independence in their intimate family, their extended family and their college. That independence promotes a pure democracy within the *oikos*, college decisions being made by the consensus of its members. The life of a college, though, is far broader than those decisions, with opportunities for independent initiative in intramural apartment offices, studios and shops serving college members, in the college studio, kitchen, laboratory and farm, in the semi-public performance and dining halls, and in extramural and public college shops. The reputation which an individual establishes in these other lines of work in the college, limited to their college in comparison, earns them respect when college decisions are made. A similar dynamic is seen in small town meetings when the opinion of the local electrician or the local plumber is sought over outsiders and over those of greater renown in areas other than the specific expertise required at that point. The humble workman shines for a day while the luminaries sit in the shadows.

It might be that those who work in the college shops might not be appreciated for all they do to build up the good name of the college, as the retail worker of today is paid a pittance for all they do to build the brand of an alien corporation with their neighbors. Those who work outside the college might be called impractical, even if esteemed, because their families and friends do not even try to understand what they do for their wages, as is the case today for the commuter. Yet they would be appreciated and respected fully by those they serve and it is that respect which is most important for the broader world of which the college, for better or worse, is a part.

For by working with the public, they provide a harmonious interaction of the rural college with its urban village, thus ending the ancient conflict between country and city. Indeed, there are not, any longer, city people separate from country people, but all are country people living in colleges within a city. This harmony is enhanced by the fact that, though country people may venture out of their *oikos* to enjoy the benefits of their urban *polis* or to offer their own goods and services at the gates of the *oikos* or beyond, they need not do so. The *oikos* is kept from being made a servant to the *polis* because of that lack of necessity. As in their namesake institutions, one can live a very full life in a household college without venturing beyond its walls.

Still, their blissful, sequestered life may be brought to a stressful, puzzling end by the loss of their communal ownership of the college's land. Our smaller households suffer this same distressing end through foreclosures, so we should understand that our personal power and liberty depends upon each of us having an inviolable legal right to live in our homes. That right is perniciously and persistently undermined and attacked by the current notion of property. We therefore need next to consider a revised and more amenable definition of property, one made to satisfy an old Populist demand alluded to earlier, that of ending *alien ownership*. To those readers unfamiliar with the term, the absentee landlord may be offered as an example. These landlords take money out of the local economy in the form of rent and take citizenship away from local people by eviction. Mortgage lenders are another form of absentee landlord, with mortgage payments and foreclosures in the place of rent and eviction. Retail and supermarket chains are other examples of absentee owner, sucking money out of the local economy and causing local citizens to lose their shops, their jobs, their income and, eventually, their residence and citizenship. If they remain, they have been demoted by this alien ownership into renters, borrowers, consumers and employees.

In the late nineteenth century, alien ownership was seen mostly in the out-of-state ownership of land and of the railroads, but has never been limited to these. Yet in whatever form it has appeared over the years, alien ownership has always been the chief complaint of the Populists, its abolition their premier goal. Populist rhetoric against Wall Street is rooted in its trading primarily in regional and national companies which are necessarily alien to the local communities where they own manufacturing, distribution and retail facilities. Even if there is a local company on the Wall Street exchanges, the intention of its listing is to invite alien ownership. The money question for Populists is decided also in favor of locally owned money and against alien finance. Since the supply of gold is global and therefore alien, Populists opposed it being used to restrict local money supplies. Silver was only marginally better and could only be so for a time. Once the market for silver was effectively cornered, owners of silver became alien owners of local money. Similarly, the Federal Reserve System was anathema to Populists because it gave lenders from outside a community the power to create and thus to own money needed within it. Worse, basing that money on reserves composed mostly of Treasuries, as is the case today, keeps that federal debt from being retired and permits an effective alien ownership of our sovereignty. Instead of these monetary policies, Populists favored the United States Notes of their

Greenback forebears and added the Sub-Treasury Plan to create money locally from granary receipts. Again, in transportation and communications, the Populist call was for an end to alien ownership of railroads, telephone and telegraph, to which modern Populists would add television and internet. A Populist today would also insist that the utilities be owned and operated by local governments rather than be controlled by alien-owned corporations or "authorities".

The implication for land ownership is that no one should own land on which they do not dwell; land should not be private property — as that term is currently understood — but be the domain of a college or a level of the *polis*.[1] Controlling stock ownership in a local company should also be local, lest that company seize power over the local people. Since the land which forms the site of a local company will not get up and move away, since it cannot then be exported, members of the *polis* with sovereignty over that land should be the only ones to own controlling shares in the company,

---

[1] See [GEORGE Progess&Poverty] for an analysis of the economic ills brought on by land ownership and a remedy consisting of undoing that ownership through a single tax on private gains from that property.

as mentioned earlier for the college. The *polis* can then be considered as an owner of half of each company as it supplies not only that site, but also sends the provisions which find their way to that company through each college which invests in it, and therefore is entitled to half of any sales generated by it. This revenue would then be the main way that money issued by the *polis* in the provision finds its way back to the *polis*.

Private ownership prevents this flow of money in a self-replenishing cycle, subsidizing alien ownership with the benefits of locating in a community, including its local material and labor. The people get nothing in return but highly begrudged, if not exempted, taxes. Yet these companies have the gall to suggest that they pay for these benefits with the supposed ability they grant to local government to impose greater taxes on the people, with one device or another, ostensibly from their good graces in granting low-paying jobs to those who became unemployed from the exercise of monopolistic practices enabled by their alien ownership. From such deceit, handsomely packaged by the political parties financed by these alien corporations, comes the absurd theatrics of sovereign domains competing for the privilege of alien exploitation with ever more generous tax breaks. If the provision and an ownership by local domain had no other benefit, it would be well worth ending this business of paying to slap ourselves.

Private property in land and companies should therefore be eschewed here because it promotes alien ownership. Deeds and shares in individual hands are easily exported into alien hands by those individuals becoming alien when they move away or by them willing their shares to an alien heir. It is essential, then, to the maintenance of local control that such ownership be prohibited, indeed, ruled out by the legal structure of stock ownership. Thus, the first revision to the concept of property is that there should be no property in land, but only domain, and that controlling property in local industry and companies should be limited to the local colleges. The first revision will be made clearer when we apply the notion of domain to the *polis* in discussing the village in the next chapter. The second revision is best left to our discussion of popular capital in a later chapter.

The Village

The Village

The first thing we need to define, before we can specify the proper structure of the *polis*, is the nature of a citizen. In *The Politics*, Aristotle simplifies the idea of the *oikos* so that the only legitimate household consists of a family with land and independent means along with its servants, headed by the head of that family, who is then the prime citizen. The male heirs are also considered citizens, by prospect, as they may become heads of families with land and independent means. Thus, the women and slaves are excluded from citizenship, the case of the worker being problematic because of his dependence on wages and his lack of land. The popular capitalist conception of the *oikos* turns this reasoning on its head by providing each person a means which is independent from wages, service, marriage or inheritance, as well as dominion of land in common with other members of their college. This brings all people equitably into the citizenry.

At the same time, it presents the problem of deciding which citizen rights to give those residents who, because of age or recent arrival, are not to be trusted with the attendant responsibilities. Equity would suggest, however, that whatever the term and conditions are for the citizen-in-training, they should be the same for a child as for an immigrant. If we have the children wait until age seven to vote in an election, we should not allow an immigrant to cast a ballot within a few years of coming into the state. If we provide for a child by way of their parents, extended family and college, we should also provide for a new immigrant in the same way. And if we hold back a child's personal portion in trust for their coming of age, so should we reserve an immigrant's personal portion in trust for their becoming a full citizen.

The only real distinction which can be made is at the level of the *oikos*: children born to members of a college are automatically members of that college, while immigrants who have attained full citizenship, along with other prospective members, must be approved by some means. A very reasonable one would be the unanimous approval of a quorum of current college members who are also citizens. This preserves the power of current citizens over their established homes while rewarding immigrants for their long devotion to their adopted country with a greater status as citizens. However, if a college fails to hold a quorum of citizen members, then non-member citizen residents, either immigrants or sojourners, should be admitted as members without approval until it does,

Students of history will recognize this as a solution, in the *oikos*, of the *pocket borough* or *rotten borough* problem of representative government based on land. The highest level of the *polis* can establish a quorum for colleges so that attrition and manipulation in a college does not result in a single person or small clique owning the same citizenship power of its fully populated neighbors. Those without a college, whether recent immigrants or sojourners, can become members of a depleted college over any objections from a single owner or a small clique. In this manner, a rotten college is filled and the power of a closed club of its elite is dissipated into the sea of new residents. Short of this extreme of vacant estates with manorial lords, colleges have a strong incentive to admit new members as each resident comes with a contribution to the college funds.

In determining the length of residence for citizenship and eligibility for office, it is useful for colleges to have a clear separation between internal and external interactions, between the community within a college and the community beyond it. With the walls of the college containing the farm and the collegial community, and each level of the *polis* adopting the same approach, like the walls of medieval towns, it is straightforward to track weekly locations. We can then stipulate the term of citizenship fairly, with those fully and faithfully staying and living with their families, friends and neighbors more quickly gaining citizenship and the right to run for office than their gallivanting house-mates. We may thus require our seven years as three-hundred and sixty-five weeks of residency in that *polis* to which a citizenship applies. By applying this same rule for each level of the *polis*, we can prevent *carpetbagging* and celebrity politicians taking over from the locals.

There will therefore be some number of people in transition, from family to family, from college to college and from country to country. As such, there will be need for housing arrangements suitable for their transitory circumstances, as well as for travelers who are maintaining their housing at home. This can be done fairly by assigning a one-quarter provision per person for food to wherever they are staying (college or inn), by assigning a quarter-provision for rent on each regular room (half-provision for double-sized and three-quarter provision for triple-sized) which the traveling group is occupying in both college and inn, and by assigning a quarter-provision for furniture, bedding and clothing in each regular bedroom (three-quarter provision for the triple-sized bedrooms) in the apartments being used by the traveling group wherever they are staying, college or inn. When away from home, the room portion would be used by the inn to provide bedclothes for the night, laundering of the traveling clothes for their departure, and clothing for each day they stay at the inn, thus saving the travelers the trouble and expense of packing and transporting their own clothing. By sending their measurements and style preferences ahead to the places where they will be staying, the travelers can be assured of having clothes which fit them for the length of their stay.[1] As for the length of stay, that can return to a more civilized fortnight, or two weeks, because the provision relieves the pressures of having to return to work after too short a vacation or from having to leave the college at all for performances or games played by the children. Nonetheless, if there is a reason for a shorter stay, each weekly amount can be prorated by one-seventh in order to arrive at a daily amount.

Yet the foregoing assumes that the structure of the *oikos* and the notion of land as a basis of citizenship rather than property is established. Under the current *land as property* regime, a different mechanism should

---

[1] Such a service might be a wise business move for a large hotel or hotel business in the present day as they could use their large laundering facilities for entire wardrobes of their guests, rather than just a few items chosen *a la carte*, achieving even greater economies of scale than with bedding, towels and wash cloths.

be used during the transition or simply as a reform and improvement. That mechanism should, at least, prevent the shackles of debt being placed on the people as a precondition to landed citizenship. We would have achieved no liberation from poverty and no improvement over anarchy if we force the people into indebted servitude before they gain the right to call home the land on which they live. The mortgage loan should be abolished and everywhere replaced with an honest and simple contract to transfer the equity in house and land quickly and certainly from the seller to the buyer.

This contract, the Square Real Estate Deal, achieves those ends by transferring a percentage of real estate equity each period, instead of a percentage of its sales price, to the *resident buyer*, who is the purchaser of the real estate under this contract. Thus, the value of each coupon, the value of the equity held by the sellers (comparable to the remaining principal on a mortgage) and the value of the equity held by the *resident buyer*, are all kept current with the same present valuation of the real estate being purchased. For that purpose, and to ensure tax equity, the tax assessment is used as that present valuation. Note that the purchase of the real estate is not complete until the *resident buyer* has bought all of the equity, so that they are never left with a cash obligation in excess of the value of their equity. In modern parlance, they can never be *underwater* on a Square Real Estate Deal. In addition, all of the fees associated with the transfer of real estate to the resident buyer, including administration, legal, listing, sales, taxes, maintenance and insurance are paid in increments based on the total equity value at the time of each coupon purchase, and paid per equity shares by each current holder of an equity share. Thus, all of the parties can continue in this contract despite the vagaries of market pricing and, should the *resident buyer* wish to leave, they can transfer their role as a *resident buyer* to another party — found by a new *sales agent*, replacing the *sales agent* who brought the current resident buyer into the contract — or the property can be auctioned off, the net proceeds from that sale being distributed according to the percentage equity shares at the time of the auction.

Unlike home buyers who finance their purchase with a conventional mortgage loan, the *resident buyers* under the Square Real Estate Deal do not have to take a position committing themselves to a price for the life of the contract. Thus, not only is a *resident buyer* assured of never being *underwater,* the seller is not paid for an equity share until that share is bought. Though the seller does not receive the full sale price of the property when a buyer moves in, that sale price would be a fraction of the stated price if the buyer also completed their side of the transaction at the same time. The seller is not hurt by having to adhere to the same payment arrangement as the buyer but simply deprived of an unfair advantage of cashing out at the current price. Moreover, that unfair advantage discourages some buyers or their lenders from bidding for a house at an unsustainable price. With many buyers discouraged or unwilling to commit to payments far into the future for a house which will, in their judgment, not retain its value after a few months, the unfair advantage on a sale can become an extreme disadvantage when trying to make such a sale. An unlikely advantage is no advantage at all. Holding coupons for future sale thus poses no disadvantage for the seller while removing the disadvantage for the buyer which the mortgage loan poses.

Those coupons, in fact, hold the key for a seller to cash out if they so desired. Since the Square Real Estate Deal provides a secondary market in these coupons, the seller can simply sell them there. Purchasers of the coupons would be, in effect, real estate futures investors who would be finding a market price for the present value of these fractions of equity values. Conversely, sellers can hold onto some coupons and benefit from any increases in the sale price of their former home while bearing the risk for any decreases. With any gains or losses from the fluctuations in value of the property being proportionately represented in each equity stake, the Square Real Estate Deal would not be leveraged and therefore would not contribute to the speculative booms and busts of the mortgage loan. This greater stability in housing prices, and the ability of sellers to gradually extract property value from a sale over time, allows citizens to preserve their control over their own homes and equity even if required to move before completing the Square Real Estate Deal.

These features, alone, do not reduce the onerous thirty or fifteen year terms of the conventional mortgage loan. Though seven years is sufficient time for buyers and sellers to ride out fluctuations in housing prices, while allowing the buyer to have a reasonable degree of confidence that they will have the income to make the last payments, there is a disadvantage to adopting that term unilaterally. The longer terms of the mortgage loan make higher housing prices more palatable to potential home buyers, thereby inflating those same prices and giving other home buyers the impression that the longer terms are necessary. This is what makes easy payment plans so attractive to retailers. They are able to extract more money from you by noting how little you would pay per month. They know you would balk at the full price, so they break it up into more *manageable* chunks that you might think you could digest. Enough people fall for this trick, and do so regularly, that the prices of the goods to which it is applied can rise to a large multiple of what the cash-on-hand market would bear. These self-fulfilling prophecies can only be broken with laws, crashes or perhaps from a cultural recognition that comes from little poems like this of mine:

Simple Simon Explains Consumer Credit

Simple Simon met a pie man going to the fair.
Said Simple Simon to the pie man,
> "May I taste your wares?"

Said the pie man to Simple Simon,
> "Each pie's four hundred bucks."

Said Simple Simon to the pie man,
> "I'm kind of down on my luck."

Said the pie man to Simple Simon,
> "Hey, no problem man.

You can eat the pie if you sign right here
> for the Simple Payment Plan."

Simple Simon looks askance and asks,
> "What did you say?"

The pie man smiles and explains,
> "You pay no money today.

And every week, only four bucks,
> until you're old and gray."

"Why so long?" asks Simple Simon,
> "I should be done within two years."

Replied the pie man, "It's not like that.
> There's an interest rate, I fear."

Simple Simon thinks a while and then gives his response,

The Village

"I'm simple, true, it is my name, but any fool can see
that it's the loan you're offering
      which makes your pies so dear."
The pie man is experienced and is quick to sport a sneer,
"I have my costs. Why, the price of fruit
      has been doubling every few months
and with labor troubles at the Little Red Hen's,
      flour is not cheap."
Simple Simon thought again, as he does for everything,
for he doesn't know what the smart folks know
      who call him a simpleton.
"Perhaps these Simpleton Payment Plans
      have taken hold of late,
so that, with their weekly dough,
      the pie men bid up the flour and fruit."
The pie man sighed for his wounded pride,
      then snidely gave his final pitch,
"I suppose there are people for whom my pies
      are just too rich."
But Simple Simon had no pride; no image did he seek.
As he waved good-bye to the pie man,
      he saved four bucks every week.

                — *C. P. Klapper, July 14, 2010*

Another version of this trick is to be found in consumer credit cards. Similarly to the thirty-year mortgage, these loans are secured by credit scores and based upon an extrapolation of current income and living expenses into the future. Very few people, if any, intentionally filch on their debts, but most people are optimistic to a fault. When their optimism is misplaced, then they become a credit risk to lenders who were more than willing to share in that optimism and prospective business when granting a loan. This risk is therefore greater when the term of the loan is extended further into the future, irrespective of the credit rating and its indication of how well expectations of ability to pay had been borne out in the past. The seven-year term which we apply to the Square Real Estate Deal could then be as judiciously applied to limit the speculative excesses of both revolving credit and mortgage loans.

The reform of a statutory, if not conventional, seven-year mortgage loan would then reduce housing prices to truly manageable levels while simultaneously reducing credit risk on those loans. The prices of consumer goods would likewise decline while reducing the risk from revolving credit. However, without those reforms, the best that a Square Real Estate Deal can do is to reduce the leveraging in its own market space, which the lack of such reforms limits. Likewise, lack of property tax fairness disadvantages Square Real Estate Deals by exempting taxes on the implicit, but effectual owners of equity, being the mortgage lenders, even as they have exempted the seller from those taxes by closing the deal with a lump sum payment of an inflated sale price. However fair the Square Real Estate Deal actually is, the loss of this apparent advantage of being exempted from taxes on their old property is a difficult objection to overcome. The seller will likely persist in their delusion that the inability of prospective buyers to commit is the reason their property is not selling, or high interest rates, or curb appeal, or any of a number of other reasons but the actual one: their price is too high, making the property taxes too high, along with the high mortgage payments, with no relief for any prospective buyer except the highly unlikely scenarios of the bubble rapidly expanding so they can flip the property, of a sharp reduction in local property tax rates, or of them receiving a huge windfall of cash that can overcome their folly in paying too much for a house. Yet to match the terms of the Square Real Estate Deal to those of a conventional mortgage in apparent affordability would defeat its purpose.

Let us assume that, despite these disadvantages, the Square Real Estate Deal has been used enough to convince the public that the mortgage loan should be abolished. This reform can and should be followed by a gradual reduction of the term of this type of real estate contract to about seven years. If the residential age for citizenship is established at roughly seven years and ownership of real estate is limited to citizens, then a seven-year Square Real Estate Deal would, in the case of children, correspond to full landed citizenship by the time they reach their teenage years. The process can begin on their seventh birthday with a seven-year Square Real Estate Deal allowing them to buy into their share of the family apartment or house by their fourteenth birthday. The provision payment would be available for this purpose and could be supplemented, if necessary, by parents and other family members. A similar dynamic in the immigrant communities would

The Village

allow new citizens to establish households in a new country, using the communal bonds they had in the old.

For our purposes, the Square Real Estate Deal is primarily a tool to help form households, be they colleges, neighborhoods or hamlets. By treating both current residents and new members fairly with respect to their property, the Square Real Estate Deal facilitates the closer union of constituent residents and housing into a household or *oikos* without having to first or to ever construct a communal architecture that would obviate separate pricing for family dwellings. Land, stores and studios can be transferred to common use by the Square Real Estate Deal as well, probably more easily as there is less of a desire for an exclusive control of current commercial enterprises than for one's home. The shops, studios and offices which were extensions of the home, which would have been there but for zoning, could be moved to their proper location when a domain is established for the college, the facilities housing them then being made available for more common purposes.

Once the concept of land as the domain for a college of citizens is established, the regularization of the college described earlier can occur. Similarly, those houses where the visitors, immigrants and sojourners are staying can be made into standard visitor hotels, immigrant houses and sojourner inns, though these are more transient communities and cannot be run entirely like colleges. To ensure continuity, their administrations must be staffed and their operations regulated by law and the village. Nonetheless, the residents of each of these should have first refusal in the hiring for any position in their own house for which they are qualified. The immigrants, especially, require this because they do not receive the full provision and, because they would otherwise be abused as *guest workers*, are not permitted employment outside of their house. However, those houses include the home and street shops, so that inhabitants of the apartment or house, respectively, are the only ones who can run and profit from those. Thus, even the more marginal dwellers in and visitors of a village are given the dignity of not being treated like mere consumers and employees.

There will, however, still be consumers and employees, as residents and visitors will both want

The Village

more than mere survival, demanding luxuries and seeking the means to pay for them. Yet, there is another reason for the houses to be joined together in a village. For though the colleges should be self-sustaining, and the administration of the more transient houses required an efficiency that should make them self-sustaining, there will still be some days where one house or college has less water, fuel or electricity than they require, and another house or college can supply the deficiency. This ability to share is more reliable when the utilities are connected to a grid for the village, with the village itself maintaining a supply of water, fuel and electricity. Going through the village is necessary for the sharing of water, because the excess from the colleges and houses will be unfiltered, requiring passage through swamps or through the ecosystem of the village farm before an equivalent quantity of water is available to supply those houses and colleges demanding additional water.

The access to the village grid would most reasonably be through the alleys forming the borders between the colleges in a block, with the visitor hotels, immigrant houses and sojourner inns being structurally the same as colleges. Given the size of each college, one hundred acres, the blocks should be as small as possible while providing flexibility of direction. Thus, the blocks should consist of three colleges with a small internal border area, in a design I describe elsewhere, as it is beyond the scope of this book.

The external border area is the street, which can be covered and for which there is no need for roads. Anything needing to be delivered to a college can be transported, within the neighborhood, several yards or a few miles, if need be, by means of hand trucks, pallet jacks and forklifts.[1] Without roads, the utilities grid can then connect to the blocks at junctures underneath the streets. A circumferential train route would serve longer

---

[1] This is, in fact, how most products are delivered over the last half mile or so from motor truck to their final delivery location. The larger rigs are not at all suitable for local delivery. I have witnessed several instances of tractor-trailers getting stuck on their way to or upon leaving a local drop-off of a small load, something which could have been delivered with a van. The drivers, defending the honor and reason of their employers, insist that it is more economical to make a hundred deliveries countrywide from a large truck than to use vans to make a local delivery of a van-sized load, ignoring the large costs in time and frustration they just experienced, as well as alternative methods of shipping. From such ludicrous arguments come the insistence on ever-widening roads and ever-narrowing sidewalks when, in fact, the exact opposite is necessary.

The Village

hauls, with stops serving the outer neighborhoods, organized into *wards*, and the village wall[1] underneath the train would serve the transport of utilities between the wards and between the village and the wider world. A watercourse around the central village farm would provide an adequate and pleasant form of transportation in the village interior.

The streets are mostly filled with college shops, for which a common currency is needed. The next essential function of the village is therefore to issue its own money, a village currency, to facilitate commerce on its streets. One need not look very far to see the dire consequences of failing to do this, of relying on remote governments or self-interested lenders for an adequate local supply of money. Though there are a few forward-looking communities which have their own currency, the balance of the municipalities are in chains of their own making while they fret over austerity budgets,

---

[1] The village wall also enables the separation and security once provided by distance and slower means of travel. Indeed, it is necessary for this purpose alone, as can be seen by invasions of our local commerce by national and regional chains, drive-by shootings and drive-in home invasions. All of these atrocities would be unthinkable to the era before the automobile. They can all be ended by the building of village walls which deny access to motorists.

paying their civil servants with taxes they collect or any subsidies they can beg or borrow. The whole traumatic dilemma would disappear, as if by magic, if they reasserted their sovereign right to issue their own money. They could pay their civil servants with that money and collect dues, fees and taxes only in that same money, being sure to build a deficit sufficient to support the local commerce. It should be noted that this is the exact opposite of the present concern.

Next, the village needs to provide places for its people, as individuals, intimate and extended families, and colleges, to keep their money. The postal banks in the apartments and the colleges serve the needs of all but the colleges. The postal banks serving the colleges should be close enough to be convenient and be large enough to be efficient. For this and for other purposes of the village, it is useful to conceive of public *colleges* where these purposes are achieved with sufficient building and grounds. These colleges are free standing, with the street on every side, so that it can be accessed from every direction. The distance should also be kept small, by each serving a ward of ten blocks with a total of twenty-seven residential colleges, a visitor hotel, an immigrant house and a sojourner inn.

As the college providing banking is the same size as other colleges, there is no reason not to have it implement related functions. Since currency can be shipped to and from this college, other things can be shipped and received; it is a post office. Since most contracts involve money transactions and since the law imposes fines for various infractions, we should include legal functions in the purpose of this college; it is a court. The need to store legal records, as well as statutes and implementing regulations, adds the categorization and storage functions; this college is the central library. Since the bank and the court need secure transport of things, it is reasonable that this college should similarly aid in securely transporting people; the college is a station and a passport office. The information stored in the library and sent by post is enough to suggest that more modern communications should be based in this college; it is a hub for the internet, for telephones and for television and radio. It would have the broadcast and cellular towers, and the computers to store the data.

Of course, the post office has performed many of these functions over the years, with others being suggested, as the Populists did with their proposal for postal banks. Nonetheless, the name *post office* might not be an adequate name for what is a college of all official matters. Perhaps a disciplinary designation is more appropriate, as we would expect that a college for which legal argument played a key part to resemble Inns of Court, those being both schools and professional associations. As its functions are predominantly social, we will designate this public college to be a College of Social Sciences.

In like manner, we extend the implementation of the civic duty of providing medical care from a hospital into an institution performing the broader function of caring for plants and beasts, as well as Man. Zoological and botanical gardens inhabit the inner space of this College of Biological Sciences, as much for the comfort of the sick as for the education of the student. Nor need the studies be limited to failures of living organisms, as this college will also pursue advances in agriculture and husbandry, seek greater sustainability in our ecosystems and examine the promises and pitfalls of nutrition. This college will both train doctors for when we are ill and prevent, as much as possible, that occurrence. Providing this free of charge would obviate any worries about so-called *medical costs* and sets aside any fears about not attracting qualified doctors and nurses in poor villages. When one's training is freely provided, there is no need to serve the wealthy first, no need to earn enough to pay the medical school loans. Such is the case whether it is established as part of the village as here described or as municipal medical departments serving the health needs of the public without charge or middlemen.

The next area to consider is, at once, the most spectacular and the most mundane. The maintenance of the infrastructure is the immediate public need. Skill in the building trades, though greater than people think, is too familiar to excite the imagination. The latest marvel of technology, though more prosaic an application of science than thought, dazzles where it does not inspire. Each is a work of engineering, borne upon the devices of physical science. So the public works of a village lie at the heart of the College of Physical Sciences.

From these more direct public missions comes the need for more abstract tools: mathematics, computer programs, linguistics, philosophy and symbolic logic. Eschewing the empiricism of science proper and more formal than the arts, these disciplines occupy a space beyond, within and between the disciplines of the other colleges, in abstract thinking. So we may simply call this public college: the College of Abstract Thought.

The cultural life of the village grows from roots in each residential college, as also do the sciences and abstract thought, but without a practical public purpose. Yet, by not being practical, the public purpose of art is all the more important. Every village can have quality science and abstract reasoning, but what distinguishes one village from another are the unique products of its painters, actors, sculptors, musicians, composers, poets, authors, choreographers, dancers and singers, as well as the critical selection of these works in each ward, showcased in the College of the Arts.

The remaining public activity we ensconce in a hundred acre facility and grounds is competitive sports. To the games and contests between the teams of each ward is added the associated training, as well as other physical activities giving individual enjoyment and relief from stress. Though these activities might be pursued at home, a *College of Athletics* can provide a more suitable environment and better facilities for each athlete's chosen sport than what their residential college can be expected to provide, and only a public college can devote its interior acreage to stadiums, tracks and playing fields of every kind, without any concern about growing food or raising animals.

Individual villages might have other divisions of their tasks into subject matter, but whatever these might be, and for the division just presented, there will be one authority as to the truths upon which the operations of a village is based. Each of the public colleges will have their own library, their own classrooms for instruction, their own laboratories of a kind for exploration, yet in the official college should reside the authority to grant the certification of knowledge in their subject matter, as that knowledge would have first been established by law. This may strike some as odd when applied to some academic subjects, but what is law but the official truth in the subjects which it addresses. Academics are called before legislatures to testify on the established truth in their subject whenever pertinent to a regulation or a bill. A far more consistent application of that established truth would result from establishing the official truth as it is being resolved in academia. There would be even far more consistency by formalizing that resolution in a system of academic courts, than in a system dependent on a questionable independence of peers. The public colleges can play a key role in establishing these truths, even as their professional staff are hired based on their understanding of what has already been established in their fields. Some may recognize in this the merit civil service advanced by the Mugwump Progressives, with the position exams replaced by academic certification. The reason for that reform, at any time, is that there is a public purpose in the proficiency of public workers.

The wards are then arranged around the quiet center of a village farm, ringed by wineries, abattoirs, packing houses, mills, silos, barns, warehouses, meeting halls, factories, offices, museums, stadiums and on-site housing for village workers. The produce from this

The Village

central land enhances the sustainability of the colleges. Natural resources are extracted from this common land, in a coordinated way, to benefit the whole village. If there are petrochemicals, these will only be extracted by a village if doing so will not endanger the water supply, because the same interests are at stake; one does not foul one's own nest. By means of its common farm and industry, as well as its purchases of other goods produced in its domain and beyond, the village keeps reserves of every kind of good needed for the survival and comfort of its citizens.

The next consideration is that of the number of wards to be included in a village. This number helps determine whether the village is a bland assemblage of interchangeable parts, similar to the tract housing of rural sprawl, or a vibrant community of diverse wards, each with its own unique character. The number of wards can also affect whether there is a unifying element to the village as a whole. To see what this might be, we need to consider first that diversity comes from the individual and that individuals are unified by the distinctive traditions they establish and maintain for their common, intimate life together. These traditions then help to form the character of the children raised within them, as a *de facto* religion. The character of a community is thus formed by its religious maintenance of its traditions and its establishment of new traditions from the individuality of its members. Their individual contributions to tradition being colored by the traditions under which they were raised, their individuality in this regard is not wholly their own, but that of their family.

The process of establishing a new tradition in a family is therefore one of blending distinct traditions, a process which radiates out with lesser intimacy to form the more public character of the extended family, college, ward and village. That is, the character of an intimate family is in the blending of the traditions each partner brings into their union from their own intimate families. Then the character of an extended family in community is a blending of the less intimate traditions of the couples in that extended family, the cousins then maintaining those traditions in the games they play, in the confidential jokes they make and in the sundry other social bonds of youth. The process continues past this point in a more disjointed manner at present, academic colleges and workplaces forming their own traditions in their own place, without much cognizance of the source of the character of their membership. As a result, their public character and those of larger communities have become disconnected from the character of the people, neither forming a truly public character nor yielding to the authority of families their own intimate traditions. This disconnection would be remedied by continuing the process of blending traditions past the family.

Thus, the character of the residential college is formed from the blending of the more public traditions of its constituent extended families. Those traditions are made comfortably public and the intimate traditions of the extended families made securely private on account of there being ninety-six such families in the college. Yet there is in the college the intimacy of common meals and common land, which gives it a unity greater than one might find in an apartment tower or a sprawl development. Next, the even more public character of the ward would be formed from the public traditions of the colleges and of individuals and families in the more transient houses. As the arrangement of the colleges and houses was in blocks of three, the number of colleges and houses within the ward is constrained to be a multiple of three. Within those choices, something within the range of a typical classroom of roughly thirty pupils is known to be comprehensible as a whole, while allowing each pupil to know each of their classmates as individuals.

Within the ward, the twenty-seven colleges, and the three houses accommodating guests of one kind or another, provide a common character, a comprehensible unity and understandable diversity for the ward, such as is found in school classes of a similar size. There would then be, with twenty-seven wards in a village, enough variety in the character of each ward to be interesting without the confusion of sorting out which ward was which. Given the fluidity of movement among the wards, there could be no visitor ward, or three, to get up to the thirty count of colleges and houses within the ward, so our number of twenty-seven, for the wards in a village, can be based on just the number of colleges within a ward.

Thus far, we have presented the opportunities for enterprise by intimate and extended families, as well as the common work which can be done within colleges and villages. We should note, in passing, that it is not the individual as individual which conducts business, but as an intimate family; if they are able to live alone, they are their own family, and are therefore running a family business. For larger ventures, a lesser intimacy of operation ensues and, with it, the need for objectivity which characterizes the village bureaucracies. Indeed, it is often remarked how the large corporations resemble the large governments in the size and impenetrability of their bureaucracies. Without approaching the size of any such behemoth, we can see that their formal structure establishes a routine fairness, a mechanical objectivity which gives every person the same treatment for equal adherence to the rules.

When this objectivity is applied to the hiring process, it is the *merit civil service*, highly revered for its purity of individual opportunity. Unlike a family business and partisan patronage, where rank is assumed from family or party rank irrespective of competence, position in the merit civil service is set by competence objectively determined by scores on pertinent exams. Moreover, strict adherence of civil servants to the paths selected by the people assures that their work will be a popular enterprise. It is therefore to this model that we turn when creating a formal structure for residential colleges to pursue opportunities.

That is, the public colleges establish, for each product in their subject area and noting each new invention involved, manufacturing procedures and positions, along with the requirements for each of these positions, so that the residential colleges can invest in the companies according to what the companies produce or can vote to change what is produced. Rather than the mock entrepreneurial units of large companies, divorced from any popular control and expecting initiative from servile employees, we have in the mutual enterprises of colleges both popular control and collegial initiative, a truly popular enterprise. We then describe, in the next chapter, this enterprise as a form of capitalism, indeed its truest form.

Popular Capital

The terms *popular* and *capitalism* have many definitions in common usage which only confuse any discussion of *popular capitalism* and thereby of the *popular capital* which is key to its formulation. Clearer definitions need to be presented.

First of all, popular is that which is by, for and of *the people*. The term *the people* denotes a group of living persons, not just individually, but together with their families and friends forming their closest communities. From our discussion above, those communities are the *oikoi*, the households, the colleges of extended families, living on and off of the land, as we advocated above. These are closest to individuals and most amenable to their control, as well as being most protective of their interests and their personal power. To strip an individual of their household, or to limit the size of the household to a nuclear family, is to leave that individual unable to fend for themselves against the more extensive power of corporate and elected governments. The power of the individual is inseparable from the power of the household so that popular capital would be capital owned by the colleges of a village for the benefit of their individual members.

We next turn to *capital* and adopt its functional usage, freed from the context of currency and exchange in which it is so frequently and erroneously set. That is, capital is the expensive machinery used to augment production in an enterprise. Because of the expense of this machinery, beyond the capability of any one participant, the enterprise is necessarily a cooperative one, both in its financing and in distributing its rewards. By extension, capitalism is a political economic mechanism whereby companies acquire machinery through shared investment and share some portion of

Popular Capital

the revenue[1] from its use with the investors according to their individual share in those investments, specifically their shares in their respective joint-stock companies.

We may also adopt the current practice of considering labor, as arranged for production, to be human capital, so that the investment in gathering a workforce and in paying their salaries is also a capital investment along with whatever equipment or machines are gathered in advance of production. Likewise, any license to use a patented or copyrighted idea in production is idea capital, the license payments being capital investments. Even fuel and other resources are

---

1 The use of the word *profit* with any degree of clarity assumes a clear definition of the word *cost*, yet the latter word is bandied about and distorted so much in the presence of the former to be nearly meaningless in that context. Preferential salaries given to incompetent friends or extorted by labor unions are sanctified as *labor costs*. The whims and conceits of a company founder or its current leaders, often directed toward cornering a market, are declared *research costs*. The increased prices of medical equipment that result from the manipulation of their demand, the hiking of tuition by a cartel of medical schools in league with a physicians union, hyperinflation in medical fees caused by health insurance, and the monopolistic pricing of drugs from the unconstitutional intellectual property in medicinal formulae, are all included in the supposedly inevitable *health care costs*. Each of these make any calculation of profit highly dubious for investors and for our purposes here. What is clear, though, is what has been stated: investors receive a portion of the revenue received by the company in which they invested.

considered resource capital, while raw material and parts stored away in inventory are considered working capital. Indeed, anything bought and used in production is part of the process used to transform those inputs into the product, and is therefore a capital investment.

Moreover, the machinery which is the exemplar of capital is often leased, rather than purchased. Even if purchased outright, its value is depreciated over time to account for its replacement cost. With the cost spread over time, we cannot distinguish between capital proper and other inputs on the manner of payment. These may be just as frequent as the lease payments on machinery. This allows us to get at the root of the matter to define capital as the regular investment in an enterprise which grants a right to the regular revenue which results from the production which that investment enables. We note that this removes a difficulty of the ownership of capital in shares of stock, namely the separation of risk and reward, of investment and return, of bearing responsibility for the maintenance and operation of an ongoing industrial concern and possessing the privilege of dismantling it to sell off its parts. With our new definition of capital, the rights of stock ownership come not only with privileges but responsibilities. That alone should protect communities and workers at a plant from the accounting whims of stock markets.

Putting the two concepts together, we define *popular capital* as being the shares which the colleges of a village own in joint stock companies in order to maintain investment in the daily operations of these enterprises and receive a corresponding portion of their revenue. The notion of property which comes out of this definition and that of the college is that the land and those things rooted in the land are, properly speaking, domain and not property in the usual sense. Yet in a more fundamental sense, *property* is what is legally possessed and the residents of the land possess it as legal residents and citizens, so property in land and in any company based on that land is domain. This is recognized in the right of the town government to issue ordinances which businesses operating in that town must follow. Irrespective of the advisability of those ordinances or of town residents using ordinances to assert their property rights in their town as the location for businesses, those rights remain and their violation a valid source of grievance.

The elaborated notion of *private property* is also not as limited as in general usage, because the notion of *privacy* has a wider application. There is the *privacy* of the individual, but there is also the *privacy* of a couple and their nuclear family, the *private* affairs attended only by an extended family with their closest friends, and the intramural privacy of a college, which here subsumes the academic college and the close-knit small town. The divide between *private* and *public* proceeds in stages and is far more nuanced than will be admitted by the defenders of private property as an exclusive province of the individual. If the protests against actions by corporations or governments were merely *not in my backyard*, they would never rise to newsworthiness; they are, in fact, protests of *not in our neighborhood*.

A more accurate definition of *private property* would be "that which is possessed by the individual as personal belongings or by the social unit of residents of a domain by virtue of their residence in that domain". Thus, the right of each individual to their personal effects is retained, even while the right of a community to its common property is asserted, along with the right of a college to participate in companies based in their village domain. The two extremes of collective ownership of everything and the commons or industry being owned by foreign syndicates are both avoided. For the danger of individual ownership of the land and the companies located there is their becoming portable, and thus exportable to antagonistic foreign interests, in so-called *financial capital*. The Populists recognized this danger over a century ago in the possible alienation of the Pacific railroad companies[1], and many a factory town recognizes it today. However benign the intent of the original alien investors, once capital becomes mere property, to be sold to the highest bidder when an investor grows tired, wants to retire or faces default on their loans, there are no assurances that the next alien investor will be benign or, indeed, will not be downright malicious toward the local community. By

---

1 See the *Populist Party Platform* of 1896 in [HICKS.J.D.]: " The interest of the United States in the public highways built with public moneys, and the proceeds of grants of land to the Pacific railroads, should never be alienated, mortgaged, or sold, but guarded and protected for the general welfare, as provided by the laws organizing such railroads."

limiting capital to the colleges in a village, by firmly rooting capital in the domain, popular capital protects the property rights of colleges in a village to participate in the use of the village domain.

Note also that with popular capital, profit is sales revenue less investment. Since investment in these companies will be set to a fixed amount each week for each company in a village, the profit motive will be entirely directed toward the increase in sales revenue, thus by increasing the quantity, improving the quality or both of the goods produced. Gone will be the current obsession with cost-cutting which undermines our industrial base. Costs *are* capital. To remove the one is to remove the other; and to preserve the one is to preserve the other. Popular capitalism, by preserving costs, not only preserves capital, protecting the property rights of colleges, but encourages greater productivity of that capital.

We next need to consider how the endowment funding the provision of the necessities would interact with popular capital. If higher governments were allowed to choose in which local companies to invest, that would serve to undermine the local control of local companies, no less than alien ownership would. Their participation, if any, should be designed solely to provide blind investments earning revenue for their endowment or matching contributions for locally supported charities. Otherwise, the ability of higher governments to trade shares would be an avenue to favoritism and corruption. Moreover, any legislation picking which investments to make, or letting an executive branch agency do so, would allow the federal government to favor one organization over another, one mission over another and one set of adherents of a cause over another. Since every organization has these religious aspects, favoring the establishment of one over another — which trading of a government's shares in organizations would most certainly do — is, without question, an action respecting the *establishment of religion*. Therefore, in the United States, investments of the federal government can only be constitutional if they are automatic and involuntary.

That constitutional rule is based on a general principle. To be effective, the fundamental civil right of free speech requires that people be able to implement their words through the organizations they establish for that purpose, without interference or preference by any government. Applying this rule to the present context, a minimal requirement would be for each village to hold a constant percentage of the shares in its companies. Higher levels of the *polis* may have their own constant percentages according to their level, or another form of company can be created for selective investment by villages and other lower levels of government, in which higher levels of government involuntary invest, or are presumed to invest through their spending on standards, trade and infrastructure.

The constant percentages of ownership in each public company, however, are not enough to ensure government impartiality. Indeed, institutions of all kinds can use that ownership to reap governmental favors by soliciting additional *capital contributions* from its shareholders, which would then include its government. That is the terminology used by joint-stock companies. Non-profits call these funds *matching contributions* but they are the same thing. The problem is not that these contributions are made, but that they are made unevenly as one or another organization decides it is an opportune moment to extract money from its members. In order to keep the role of government from being thus manipulated, it is essential that capital contributions from all shareholders be uniform, frequent and regular. Only then can the role of government be truly blind.

It is also necessary that the total investment by a government be the same for each public stock company in its jurisdiction and thus that the number of shares be set uniformly at a constant quantity. In the case where a higher-level government is investing in companies from a variety of villages, there would also be a need to fix the number of such companies in a *village* to a fixed ratio to the number of colleges in that *village*. Otherwise, the government would be favoring companies from villages with fewer colleges per company. Even if this is not the case, there is merit in establishing such a ratio on a general basis so that more substantive productive factors can be taken into account and used efficiently by the companies, the colleges and the villages. For what a government builds is an investment, from which more populous or commercial domains reap greater benefits. The people in the small, rural states in this country have had this reason for being less than enthusiastic about expenditures on mass transit, as they should have been about the federal highway program which has benefited only large companies. The transformation from sturdily independent farmers into vassal consumers and debtors was sadly unanticipated, the inevitability of that result drowned out by the patronizing and self-serving cries of motorists to "get the farmer out of the mud" or, more to the point, "get the farmer out of the business of pulling cars out of the mud". The views of the farmer himself were, as usual, neither solicited nor heard.

We have already discussed, in the chapter on colleges, how land is not property, but *domain*, under Popular Capitalism. The notion of capital contributions described above represents a further change in our concept of property. Shares in a public company would no longer be packets of old investments whose value, at best, represents the return on those old investments.

Instead, shares would represent stewardship, a continual and regular investment in that company, for which sales revenue is the return on that investment. Profit would then be a throughput of sales above investments.

By way of contrast, the current view of profit is an end-of-accounting-period reckoning of sales minus certain costs from which some are arbitrarily excluded as *capital*. If the stockholders do not bear these costs along with the other capital costs, then a false accounting is being given with prior costs being hidden in bonds and other loans and with future costs in assets and retained, hence undistributed, earnings. This false accounting then disconnects each investor from their true return and creates a stored value in the company which may entice other investors to buy a majority stake in order to plunder it in a *hostile takeover*. We should remember that the hostility in that takeover is to the executives who have squirreled away this value as a sop to investors while depriving them of their due in dividends. By diverting stockholders away from actual returns in dividends and toward the speculative pursuit of *shareholder value* in present or future expected stock value, executives are able to wrest control of a company they were hired to manage from its own stockholders. This allows them to reward themselves, their cronies and their favored staff with large salaries and bonuses.

In the more responsible form of capital ownership espoused here, no opportunity for such a deceit presents itself. There is really no reason to create cash reserves when the necessary funds can be procured from continual investment from a large number of large households. Such ploys as increasing the *return on equity* by selling off the equity and rewarding dubious salesmanship become physically impossible if equity is conjoined with a locally rooted stock ownership. Costs cannot be outsourced, sold off, spun off or cut in any way under popular capitalism because the investments keep flowing in week after week, with the investors expecting them to be used to generate revenue in excess of that investment week after week.

We should also note that the usual defense of building up cash reserves, special capital accumulation and borrowing is that capital goods are too expensive to be paid for out of a company's cash flow, even a larger flow from continual investment. That argument ignores the notion of depreciation and the reality of machines and parts of machines wearing out upon which that notion is based. If every purchase of a capital good by a company is made gradually in the amounts of that depreciation then the cash outlays to accomplish that purchase would be affordable. This has to be the case for any capital good because otherwise the purchase of the capital good would not benefit the company on any schedule. The purchase of parts can also be phased in to correspond to the expected lifetime of those parts, even in structuring the purchase of a new machine.

The only remaining issue in this discussion of the periodic maintenance of capital is how to allow sellers of capital goods to receive their payments in full. For that we need only introduce futures contracts for each depreciation. In order to compute the price of its nth depreciation payment, we consider the price of a good $n - 1$ periods old and subtract the price of the same good n periods old. If there is not an active used goods market yet, the initial sale price can be used as the base value for the first set of terms. That base value can be adjusted for each succeeding set, based on sales of goods of similar age and interpolations of sale prices of goods differing ages in the neighborhood of the age for which we seek a price. Once established, we multiply that base value times the percentage being depreciated over the current term to come up with the price of its depreciation. Initially, those percentages can be found in percentage amortization schedules with a modest interest rate reflecting the cost of the money extended by an investor. Once an active used goods market appears, the actual depreciation in price can be used to form depreciation percentage schedules for later sales. The payment would then consist of the price of depreciation for that term, in effect the principal, plus the remaining percentage which is not depreciated times the interest rate. Each payment would be divided into one principal for the futures contract coming due and multiple interest payments for the remaining unexpired contracts. With a liquid futures market in machines and parts of various degrees of usage, a seller can sell these futures contracts and thus receive immediate payment.[1]

---

1 Note that a similar set of futures contracts and markets can be constructed for real estate sales, until those are obviated by the move from the private, and potentially alien, ownership of land

Such liquidity would also allow the buyer to sell their used goods to another company, who would then continue to pay the depreciation futures contracts. Though a college could certainly engage in this type of commodities trading, there is no reason to limit participation to them. Indeed, by allowing individuals to participate in these markets, we can achieve the desired liquidity while providing an avenue for the exercise of financial acumen which is beneficial without being controlling.

Thus, the formerly intimidating expenses of manufacturing can be easily borne by companies with relatively modest flows of investments. Maximization of profit changes critically, then, from the current practice of cutting all costs but those deemed to be

---

to colleges holding land in perpetuity as their domain. These contracts can either painstakingly determine the depreciation of each component of a house: roof, furnace, water heater, etc., or more simply pick a modest term of seven to ten years, over which some major replacements and renovations might be expected, and annually re-appraise the equity value of the house as a whole. In the latter case, the futures contracts would be for a percentage of the total equity value at that time and would correspond to mortgage payment coupons. Fairness and reason would require that the terms of mortgage loans be shortened to the same term, income projections for even seven to ten years out being problematic, never mind fifteen or thirty.

capital, to maximizing sales revenue by optimizing production to the levels best suited to the demand for the manufactured good. The ability to do this is constrained by how much capital, in the broadest sense, can be bought with the regular investments. Therefore, it follows that an equitable and free competition between companies requires that each company receives an equal investment at equal intervals.

This can be accomplished in a general way by uniformly setting the investment per share to a fixed amount, say that of the provision, and setting the total number of shares for each institution to a fixed number, say a thousand. Given that these companies are truly public companies, meant to heed the wishes of those colleges which own them, not favoring with greater pay one set of employees over another because of their membership in or relationship with the colleges with the greatest stake in those companies, they should more closely resemble public agencies, so that all employees, especially executives, would be civil servants paid on the same uniform merit pay scale as civil servants, paid by the government supplying the provision at the behest of each company's shareholders, paid with the provision as designated by those shareholders, and paid for positions with standard and objective qualifications. Since the local public resources in land, water, energy, transportation and communications will be under direct local control, with utilities charged at rates decided by local governments based on their prices in markets run by higher governments, it is only in the truly capital goods of machinery and tools used in manufacturing that we will find a business to business market.

Even there, sweetheart and backroom deals will be minimal if the governments of the higher levels of the *polis* shoulder their responsibility in regulating commerce between lower level jurisdictions, in particular by setting product standards in the capital goods trade. This is all the more necessary in managing the futures market described above, particularly when the purchase or sale of used capital goods crosses jurisdictional lines. This would open up a global futures market in capital goods depreciation payments, requiring exacting standards for the new equipment and objective measurement of wear and tear on the old.

This standardization of the products traded — which would be wisely applied in the present day to prevent adulterated, poisonous, infested, infected or dangerous agricultural products, petroleum or consumer goods from entering the trade markets — must have been what the ratifiers of the United States Constitution understood by the Congressional power "To regulate Commerce with foreign Nations, and among the several States, and with the Indian Tribes".[1] The abuse of power in coercing companies and individuals to alter their clearly local decisions to buy certain goods, which is already well beyond the scope of the commerce clause, becomes even more apparent when, in a literal reading of that clause, trade between the states is conducted by the states themselves within a federal market operated by the judicial branch under the regulations passed by Congress. The people and their companies would then have absolutely nothing to do with the operation or regulation of interstate commerce. Indeed, if the people are to realize fully the advantages of trade, comparative advantage requires companies and individuals to be separated from interstate commerce by a wall of

---

[1] United States Constitution (Article I, Section 8, Clause 3)

merchants trading foreign goods for local money. It is therefore more in keeping with the stated purpose and scope of the Commerce Clause for the judicial branch of the federal government to run a commodity exchange where state governments serve as merchants, than for any requirements or restrictions be imposed on local businesses or individuals. A more complete description of this apparatus, as well as any Constitutional changes which may be required for a federal political economy, will greatly benefit from our discussion of federalism in a later chapter and so will be postponed until later.

Our consideration of standardization of capital goods for trade, however, brings up the point of how those goods would come into being at all with business structured as presented here. Still, in all fairness to our proposed reforms, if that style of organization for companies and their operation sounds too structured to be innovative, it is because that is the nature of large organizations and of manufacturing corporations in particular. We should expect true innovation to come as it always has come: from the local artisans and shopkeepers tinkering in their studios and shops, not from faceless corporate bureaucrats. As we have found out time and time again, corporate *innovation* consists almost entirely of stealing ideas from inventors and authors — using the *assignment* and *work made for hire* provisions of patent and copyright law to claim *intellectual property* in those ideas for the corporate masters of the inventors and authors who conceived them — as well as stealing money from investors with deceptive schemes.

It cannot be too strenuously asserted that a broad dissemination of knowledge and its rapid application in industry — which was the stated intent of the so-called *copyright clause*[1] of the United States Constitution — are thwarted by the very nature of organizations, public or private, once they are given exclusive rights to that knowledge. They will use their longevity to extend those rights indefinitely in order to maximize their profit from that ownership, whether to produce or not to produce goods from that knowledge. It should therefore be the role of government, in its judicial capacity, to grant ownership of knowledge to its creators within a

---

1 Called that without, it should be noted, ever mentioning copyrights, let alone the patents it is presumed to endorse.

framework where the owners of that knowledge can profit from its widest possible use.

Thus, the role of the local university or lyceum in this respect would more properly be that of a patent and copyright office than that of an owner of *intellectual property*. Companies would pay standard fees to license their manufacture of inventions at their local university or lyceum. Those payments can then be forwarded through the judicial system to the patent and, in the case of publishing companies, the copyright owners. In addition, the local university or lyceum would pay each copyright owner for the dissemination of their ideas in each course they offer. These would ultimately be paid by the students taking each course through course fees, which would also pay for any papers and books used in the course, the copyright fees for these being paid to authors through the publisher. Trade courses would work in a similar manner, but with payments going to the inventor of new processes, thereby giving those inventors their reward without laying the heavy hand of the law upon those working their craft in the colleges or selling their wares in humble shops along the street. Similarly, the colleges should be able to teach, like their current namesakes, without intrusion or regulation, for the edification of their members. As in other matters, the college should be treated as a legal unit in matters of knowledge, free to think and create within its own collective mind. There is no plagiarism in one's own thoughts.

There is one remaining avenue for the collection of royalties for the application of new knowledge: merit employment of civil servants. Such royalties can be included in the registration fee for taking public service course examinations establishing the sufficiency and merit of one's qualifications for particular positions within public companies and governments. Obviously, examinations which test one's mastery of knowledge in the public domain would entail only a minimal, indeed nominal, fee. With copyright and patent ownership only existing for the benefit of the actual progenitors of new ideas and, in the event of their premature death, their immediate heirs, far more knowledge which has already been well publicized will be in the public domain than is the case with the corporate ownership of ideas.

Since the organizational infrastructure envisaged here actually encourages the rapid implementation and publication of new ideas along with the similarly rapid distribution of financial benefits to their authors and inventors, there is no hardship in limiting the total amount received from copyright and patent ownership. There can even be a sliding scale so that early users of a technology encourage new users to adopt it as the ideas gradually enter the public domain. Thus, the first ten million uses could be licensed at a fee of 10¢ per use, the second ten million at 9¢ per use and so on. Uses after the hundred millionth use are free, but the inventor or author then has already earned $5.5 million in license fees. This would be a great improvement over keeping technical advances proprietary until they lose their patent protection. It would lead to greater use even over the present licensing scheme for music since the license fees for covers of already successful songs would be more affordable, thus widening their use by performers who are less well known. It also avoids the hardship on students and employees of paying for ideas which have long since lost their novelty.

Popular Capitalism

Returning to the collective nature of popular capital, some may worry about the more indirect role of the individual in investing and the reduced opportunity to gain an independent wealth through investments. It must be conceded that establishment of the college domains and their ownership of village manufacturing plants prevents individuals from buying up real estate or acquiring a controlling interest in a local company. However, we have just seen how individuals can help provide liquidity to the capital goods depreciation futures markets with potential gains similar to those available on commodities markets. Other markets will present similar arbitrage opportunities benefiting those markets by adding liquidity and facilitating clearing. It should also be pointed out that financial acumen which finds a good return for the investment of college funds will profit everyone in the college through their shares. So, even though the more extreme forms of acquiring personal wealth are denied the individual in our popular capitalism, a more economically and socially beneficial form is available through these investments. Since, in Adam Smith's argument, unbridled avarice was justified by that social benefit, and not by the avarice itself, there is no reason for us, possessing a greater shared benefit and assured personal welfare under popular capitalism, to mourn the loss of an ability to more extremely satisfy our own avarice or to reject popular capitalism because we perversely wish to enable extreme avarice in a select few to the detriment of ourselves and our community.

Some may counter that large fortunes amidst poverty are both inevitable and useful. Ultimately, this claim is based on the notion that profit is the measure of all things and the venerable observation, made by such esteemed personages as Aristotle and Adam Smith, that the most profitable business activities have almost always been at the expense of the public. The first basis is not only crass, but circular, justifying profits with profits. As to the second, both esteemed authors made their observation disparagingly. To these ancient and antique critiques can be added that popular capitalism would end poverty with the provision — proving that it is not inevitable — and that the large accumulations and monopolies were never useful, the most stable profits and income having always been attained with strong community support. In this stability of profits, investments have played only a very small part, if indeed a positive one, for which it is only fitting and proper that they should receive a very small benefit.

For it has long been true that the households in the village supply the early and most loyal customers and workers. With the village land on which a factory or an office stands and its access to the transportation, natural resources and utilities of the village, customer and worker loyalty contribute more to the success of an enterprise than a few investment dollars from a remote and largely disinterested underwriter. Indeed, I would suggest that the typical municipality today fails to look after its own interest in the approval process when it does not insist on a capital stake in each such enterprise. In addition, each higher level of government has provided the broader infrastructure that allows resources to be imported and products to be exported, though this infrastructure is of less importance the more removed it is from the village.

Thus, under popular capitalism, property in a local joint stock company is constrained by the eligible owners: the colleges by choice, the village by domain and the treasuries of each higher level only in a sense so indirect that it can hardly be called property. It bears repeating, in these times of outsourcing and the suckers game of *global competition*, that if property is instead constrained to serve the local interest, then the rich cannot abscond with a village institution and ship all of its jobs out of their village, city, county, state or country. Popular capital is local capital, meaning little outside its local context.

On the other hand, we may need to provide some flexibility in allowing the adjoining villages which form a city or county to share ownership and control of a manufacturing company along their common borders. This provides an appropriate avenue for the villages, themselves, to invest in joint stock companies of their own, following the model of college investment within the village domain. Thus, if we take the city to be the next higher level of the *polis*, only villages within a city would be able to invest in a joint stock company on a city site, in the city infrastructure and organized under city law. The somewhat greater economies of scale and greater access to skilled labor of the appropriate type are then achieved without creating monopolies or public companies more powerful than their home communities and without opening any other avenue for control by a wealthy individual, who is still excluded from direct ownership.

We have mentioned before that it is essential that public companies should each have the same number of shares and that the investment per share be uniform and made frequently at regular intervals and that all workers in a public company, including and especially executive workers, should be paid according to the same pay scale as is used by civil servants. This should also apply to other public institutions which are supported on an independent basis by the households, that is, every public entity which is not already itself a government agency. There are many reasons for this, but an overriding concern is that *other people's money* is involved and therefore the reputation of all public institutions, both companies and non-profits, is at stake. Thus, rather than having the village ballet or baseball team demean themselves by plastering corporate logos, advertisements and other tokens of fealty on the walls of public theaters and sports arenas, or by begging for contributions on radio or television, a group of colleges would commit to a regular capital contribution similar to what they would invest in a more mercenary enterprise. The more modest salaries of performers and athletes would be expected, and acceptable, when they and their families are already surviving, before any stardom, and are assured of continued survival after it or without it. Then the glory is reward enough.

To provide enough regular investment at one weekly provision invested per share, we may propose that each village institution has five hundred revenue shares to be held by the colleges. The village itself will hold another five hundred non-voting, non-investment shares to reward it with half of the revenue on account of its prior investment in the facilities available at each company site and in the provision of the necessities to that institution's prospective customers and employees. Note that any general inflation would be reflected in each institution's revenue, thereby increasing the village revenue through its share in half of the proceeds, and thus decreasing the village money supply more rapidly than otherwise, all revenue going to the village being a reduction in its money supply. This then serves to curb or reverse the general inflation in the village currency. Conversely, a general deflation in the village currency would decrease the revenue of each institution, thereby decreasing the village share and slowing down any contraction of the money supply. This self-correcting mechanism does not require profits at a certain level, nor does it require a return to or an end of consumer or lender confidence, repayment of debt or balancing of budgets, to have its effect. With the provision ending poverty, only the true purpose of inflation and deflation remains: to calibrate the currency to the market.

As a result, the village institutions receive a regular infusion of funds from their investors but, because the investments are constant, without bias and without those investors being manipulated or exploited. Also, investment by government is through the people and previously built infrastructure, and hence impartial with respect to particular companies. Lastly, buying capital in increments creates a more gradual growth in profits and therefore a more gradual movement in share value. With avenues for fraud and abuse in stock trading thus limited, a free and informed stock market can be established.

Shares in the institutions of a village would be traded on the stock exchange of that same village, since only colleges from the same village as an institution would be able to purchase them. Institutions of higher levels of the *polis* would, for the same reason, be traded on exchanges of their home *polis*, at whatever level, with only the members[1] of that *polis* being able to purchase their shares. The operation of these markets is further constrained by the local scope of the money and of the provision. This constraint to the local scope, and the consequent constraints to prices, leaves no room for speculation. Instead, there is a weekly recalibration of the relative value of the various institutions, taking into account both their monetary and normative values.

For the share prices of an institution would be moved by market movements in its exchange according

---

1 Note that each member is a *polis* of the next level down for all but the village. The village, as the lowest level or root *polis*, has no *polis* of lower level, but has the college as *oikos* as its next lower level from which its membership is drawn.

to its revenue stream and the degree to which market participants tolerate or are attracted to what they expect that revenue stream to be in the near future. Thus, high share prices for an institution would be an inducement to sell, offset by an expectation of high revenue from keeping the stock for the following week. A low price would be an inducement to buy, offset by an expectation of low revenue for the following week. Since revenue cannot be lower than zero and outlay is precisely one weekly provision payment, weekly losses are limited to one provision. Weekly revenue, and thus weekly profit, is limited by the currency outstanding for that week, and thus cannot continue to expand from week to week. Past the net amount of the provision remaining in circulation, after the automatic extraction of revenue, as described for the village in the previous chapter, further increases in company revenue will deplete the money supply from earlier weeks until all of the money is removed from circulation. The maximum profit each week would therefore peak with the money supply and then subside to some share of the new money brought into circulation by the provision. With these limits on the profits and losses per share, the price movements in share prices is also limited so that, even in these stock exchanges of limited scope, no small set of colleges can manipulate the stock prices to get gains from trading at all comparable with the dividend-like gains from sales revenue. All of this is achieved by the provision and its use in the organization of these stock markets, without the heavy hand of market regulation.

It should be noted that companies with revenue per share below the provision will have stock which might not be salable at a positive price and which might not be able to be given away, thus at a zero price. In economic terms, such a stock would be a *bad*, as opposed to a *good*, and would be *sold* at a negative price. This occurs more often than is supposed, as seen by expressions such as "You would have to pay me to take that piece of junk" and by the fact that we pay people to take away our garbage. It stands to reason that negative pricing has a place in any market where items may be *bads* as well as *goods*. Moreover, by allowing negative share prices, the village stock markets can better adjust for the desire to unload losing propositions which were either supposed to be profitable concerns or are charitable organizations which the college is no longer willing or able to subsidize. At worst, a college would lose one more weekly provision for each share of an institution they unload on another college with a more sanguine or ambitious view of that institution. If it comes to it, the inability to unload shares at the price of one negative provision is a very strong inducement to organize fellow disgruntled investor colleges to change the policy or direction of the institution. For that reason, a more negative price would occur rarely if ever.

A scenario which might allow this rare event would be of monopoly or oligopoly power taking an institution on a course which is obnoxious to all but the controlling interest. In order to prevent a college being hung out to dry by one or a few colleges holding a majority stake, two limitations can be imposed on village markets. First, each college should hold no more than ten shares in any one institution, thus requiring a bloc of at least twenty-six households to secure a majority of voting shares. Second, the share price of an institution should not be more negative than, say, twelve weekly provisions and, if the market fails to clear at that price, the non-selling college with the least number of shares shall be required to buy the next offered share at the minimum price. If this process results in all of the non-selling colleges holding ten shares with no other college in that village or villages willing to bid on the next offer, then that institution would be dissolved and all equipment, unsold product, furniture and materials auctioned off, with the proceeds distributed to the remaining stockholders by share.

Thus, any attempt to rope in unsuspecting colleges to underwrite an agenda of a bloc of colleges would be mooted by that bloc assuming ownership of all of the voting shares, obviated by it expanding to fifty colleges in agreement with their agenda, or defeated by their scheme backfiring with their institution dissolved. This seems harsh from our current perspective, where such institutions form our identities by default, but with a college-centric view, they are merely the impersonal and remote institutions they always were, begging for our money through advertising and more direct means. Our athletic, cultural, artistic and religious heritage will be rooted in our colleges, with only those pursuits that are more broadly pursued venturing outside the college walls into extramural institutions. Intramural sports are more fun for more people; those who are spectators at extramural games can participate fully in the intramural games and be healthier, too. The singer, the dancer or the musician in the extramural audience, whose dreams of performing on the wider stage are vain for reasons other than talent, will find a stage in their own college. In a sense, this is all a return to our roots, to a world of gazebo concerts and village baseball teams, an infinitely more intimate experience than hearing canned music or watching a game on television.

Now, as the process of dissolution makes clear, it is essential that the operations of a public institution be performed by qualified civil servants adhering to strict regulations governing the use of institutional property. A dissolution should not be used as an occasion for pilfering what should be auctioned. This need for unflinching honesty and uprightness does not begin at the ending of an institution, but should be in place from its formation and through every stage of its operation. Indeed, it has been a common mistake to assume that corporation by-laws are sufficient to protect investors and that their greater latitude is necessary for the success of an institution, particularly for a company. This confuses the entrepreneurial efforts of an artisan or inventor with the running of a bureaucratic corporation. The artisan shopkeeper takes his risks with his money; there is no reason to replace him with a bureaucrat. Likewise, the inventor conducts his experiments on his own time using his own resources in ways a bureaucrat would never dream of. Yet, once the artisan or inventor asks or allows a company to manufacture his product or invention, there is no further need of flexibility or inventiveness. What the company is called upon to do, is to faithfully pursue the task of production by following best practices and by doing everything strictly by the book. A similar comparison can be made between a play composed and premiered in a college and its performance by a village theater. Idiosyncratic home performances need to give way to professional ones when the work enters the repertory.

The composition of the institutional staff should also be determined according to guidelines established by government at the highest level of the *polis*. Each kind of institution and mission should have a set of guidelines established for it, using job descriptions occurring in government service whenever possible. This prevents a different set of jobs and compensation being developed for institutions than for similar government work, and the corruption that would bring. In particular, management or executive work should have the same pay for the same responsibilities; if a company has a greater profit in a week or over a year, it is the result of the efforts by *all* the workers, both at that company and at its suppliers, of strong demand for its goods or services by its customers and of good fortune in finding and growing resources, not solely the result of managerial skill by the executive staff at that one company. Because of this difficulty in assessing credit or blame in the bureaucracy of any elective or corporate government, it makes sense to standardize executive pay along with the rest and to distribute the profits to its shareholders in either fiscal surpluses or dividends. By making their jobs and advancement more portable, this standardization of pay and work then provides greater flexibility for all government and institutional workers in advancing their careers. Thus the other rationale for high executive pay and severance, the degree to which executive jobs are subject to the whims of corporate politics, is mooted by their being treated and paid like civil servants.

The regulation of the job descriptions, whose necessity we have just stressed, implies a similar regulation of their requirements and the process of meeting those requirements. This has taken the form of competitive examinations in the merit civil service advocated and advanced by Carl Schurz, Theodore Roosevelt and other reformers.[1] The use of course examinations then suggests an academic partner in this process. That is, the job requirements can be specified in the manner of course prerequisites, which are courses themselves. Their fulfillment can then be shown by passing scores on the course examinations. In the case of multiple applicants for a job who both satisfied these requirements, the applicant with the highest aggregate

---

[1] In order to end patronage spoils, *merit civil service* selects workers for a position by choosing the applicants with the best scores according to an objective and unbiased measure. Its opposite is *merit pay*, where the workers are evaluated by their supervisors using arbitrary rubrics to justify managerial spoils.

score, by a predetermined aggregation, would be hired. Some flexibility in the requirements can be added, when warranted, by requiring a diploma or a degree with some concentration or major. These requirements can then be fairly set by uniformly specifying each course, diploma and degree in general use at the highest level of the *polis* where it is being used. In summary, the proper handling of government and institutional employment requires that courses be defined, exams administered and diplomas and degrees granted by government.

The compensation of civil servants would be based on the same GS model used by the federal government. The expertise level of a position is represented by the grade and the experience at that level is represented by the step. Following the same approach as was used in specifying civil service positions, we define the wages of the civil servant in a standard way, rewarding those positions with more strenuous requirements, as defined in degrees and courses and as classified in the expertise levels of the GS grades, with greater compensation. Since we view the power as no less a part of total compensation than salary, salaries increase with grade but are discounted by rank. Also, since the necessities are provided to all citizens, there is no theoretical minimum to the salaries of civil servants. Practically speaking, though, filling positions requires a minimum to induce candidates to leave the comforts of home and at least apply for any openings. Adjustments in local pay, through percentage bonuses or reductions, can be objectively made for a position whenever an opening in the village reveals a shortage or a glut of qualified applicants. The adjustments can be made until there are between three and six applicants for the job.

This pay need not and, therefore, should not be augmented with additional expenses which are not already factored into the decision to work on a given type of job for a given wage. Graveyard shifts and hazardous work should be different positions than those involving similar work during daylight hours or without the danger. We would expect, other things being equal, higher pay for a night watchman and a cop on the beat than for a daytime security guard or a policeman consigned to a desk job. On the other hand, the so-called *benefits* now regularly offered to employees would already be provided on the basis of citizenship and not of employment. For example, medical care would be a government service, primarily directed locally by municipal medical departments, with doctors and nurses on staff in each village, with additional services provided by governments at higher levels of the *polis*. All mandated staffing would be hired locally, but paid by the level of government mandating the hire.

Thus, any operating budget for labor can be balanced to any amount of revenue devoted to paying workers by solving for a GS pay scale where the inner product of an array of the number of positions at each GS grade and step with the pay scale, as a corresponding array of pay at each GS grade and step, equals the total revenue. Of course, the trivial case of a zeroed-out budget would likely cause under-staffing, even with the provision. Very low budgets would be tantamount to that, cutting programs by attrition rather than formally. Conversely, expectations of high wages and a reluctance to apply for government work for less would result in the same lack of staff for a government to implement its programs. Fortunately, replacing taxes with the endowment makes budget balancing far less important than before. As for the stability of the civil service population and the filling of openings, some federal positions may have to be adjusted at the federal level along the same lines as just discussed for the local level and for the same purposes: to discourage excess workers from flocking to one field and to encourage workers to relieve shortages in another.

In this way, the integrity of the GS grades is maintained while giving governments the flexibility they need in adjusting wages so that they can staff their departments adequately to fulfill their mission with reasonable economy. A modification is in order, however, for the treatment of steps in the GS system. Since every citizen, including each child, is assured survival through the provision, there is no need for higher income as one grows older, and hence no need for civil servants to receive a step increase just for staying in their current position. The current handling of steps is thus ill-suited to our needs under popular capitalism. The steps should instead indicate a more useful factor than chair-warming: pertinent experience.

The same structure which is used to specify requirements for a position can be used for specifying real experience in that position and pertinent experience in like positions. For each worker, each course, diploma or degree which forms the requirements of a position can be assigned a week for each week that position was held by that worker. Summing up the course, diploma and degree experience over all positions held by a worker then gives the total experience of that worker in each of those requirements. A similar exercise is often asked today of applicants for a software development position, where the applicant gives their total years of experience in FORTRAN, in COBOL, in C, in LISP, in ML, in Java and so forth. The experience applicable to a eligible position can then be calculated from its requirements by taking the minimum years of experience over all of the requirements. In the case of the programming slot example, this would indicate how many years were spent using the programming languages listed in the requirement. This number of years then constitutes the step of the applicant for that position. If the applicant has at least the step required for that position, then they become fully eligible for the position. The highest aggregate examination score on job requirement course and degree requirements among the fully eligible candidates then gains the position.

Once the position is filled the new employee is paid on the basis of the grade and step of the position, not their own grade and step. In this way the position and its compensation are both well defined. This benefits the people, who do not face expenses which are beyond what they approved or which are allocated to workers disproportionately to the skill and experience requested. It is also benefits the older civil servants, who do not face discrimination on account of the excess pay their over-qualification would otherwise have given them. It even benefits the highly qualified younger worker, in that they are given a fair chance at securing entry-level positions against older, more senior, but less qualified workers. As long as *merit* is understood to mean a better personal best score on the pertinent examinations, the workers are the most meritorious that can be assigned the work in the local labor market.

Since this merit system provides ample opportunity for workers to improve their status and professional standing, any worker who seeks to be worthy of a post in the future is treated as fairly as they should have been, given the degree to which they have succeeded in their ambitions of betterment.

It should be noted that both junior and senior positions will be required for most government and institutional work. As the elders of an agency or a company retire from the field, the more experienced workers waiting in the wings can apply for those senior positions and realize the benefit of their higher steps: they can get a raise. As with their initial hiring into that government department or institution, they are chosen for being the best qualified by aggregate score among the fully qualified candidates. Those who are too green for the position do not get considered, no matter how well they did on the examinations. Those who barely scraped by in understanding their work, though they may be considered, are at a distinct disadvantage no matter how years they have put in. In the end, the most qualified of the applicants, in this bureaucratic sense, gets promoted. Their old position then opens up for fresher faces to fill. The more senior, second-best also will likely move on to another part of the government, philanthropic and corporate world where they can realize their ambitions, freeing another spot for mid-range and entry-level applicants.

For those who find this rigid work structure too confining, or otherwise unappealing, there is the more private world of shops, studios, libraries, laboratories, communal halls for dining, edification or amusement, gymnasiums, ball fields, gardens, kitchens, farms, lounges and apartments, where one finds the college work of shopkeepers, artisans, electricians, carpenters, plumbers, handymen, tinkerers, tillers, cooks, cleaners, writers and musicians. The same work may, in many cases, be performed in the college as in the factories or government offices, but the key difference is that work in the college is done for the benefit of the college at the college's expense and accruing to the college an internal profit or a loss, while public work is done at public expense, hazarding the abuse of money or power. That is why the public work should be constrained and formal, bureaucratic, picayune and dull, while private work can be freer and more inventive.

In this regard, the record needs to be set straight as to the proper place of innovation and research. We have become too used to the corporate co-opting of these endeavors that we unthinkingly assign them to industry. Undoubtedly, this comes from the widely propagandized misconception that corporations are private entities when, as any non-partisan can plainly see, the corporation is a public institution. Indeed, modern corporations are governments which compete against the democratically elected governments for power. A key power grabbed from the people, and pressed to serve the corporate fight against democratic governments, is the power over the use of invention, in their fabrication of corporate *intellectual property rights*. The corporations' accomplice in this takeover of invention has been, in the United States, *mandatory assignment* and *work made for hire* clauses of our patent and copyright laws, respectively. Both clauses subvert the letter of the United States Constitution by granting the right to use the inventiveness of inventors and authors to their masters and not to the inventors and authors themselves.

Obviously, then, the first objective in this area of any Populist program, such as popular capitalism, is to repeal or obviate those clauses. Much of the popular capitalist program would help in obviating them so that repeal would become a mere formality. The provision of the necessities eliminates the wage slavery that has forced the inventor, the author and, that curious modern blend, the software developer to sign away their rights. Then passage of legislation to define public companies and their licensing of ideas for use in manufacturing, as in the definition of capital given above, can assure an accessible path from creation to the payment for that creation. Indeed, the establishment of public companies as college-controlled manufacturing concerns would so limit their power, and their constant though persistent investment would so limit their financial resources, that the manufacturer can no longer dictate the license fee nor lock their competitors out with exclusive licensing. However, this increased power for the individual registrant may lead to the opposite danger, that of well-connected poseurs registering patents for vague wishes in order to lock out real inventors from solving real-life problems and manufacturers willing to implement those solutions. In fact, the power of the registrant has already given legal firms the ability to lock out innovation with extortionate threats of suits over patents of this kind.

The danger of such a lock-out can be prevented, under popular capitalism, by having the manufacturing plans of the public companies reviewed to establish which patents need to be used and to establish initial mandatory licensing for an established initial quantity of the product at an initial rate. Patent judges can be appointed to perform this review using the current database of patents, thus avoiding confusion and delay from infringement cases after the fact. In fact, lawsuits and other forms of blackmail through the courts would be abolished. Their purpose will be replaced with prior judicial review, under which spurious patent registration would rarely, if ever, be effective. Initial mandatory licensing, as is currently employed for the use of music, would allow manufacturers to license patented ideas and inventors to be paid fairly for those licenses without negotiating or even meeting. Thus, even if any spurious registrations managed to slip by, they would be unable to hold production hostage. Since that is the source of the benefit for making those claims, the prevalence and costs of that danger are made minimal.

It is worth noting that this initial mandatory licensing under popular capitalism also ensures wider adoption of those ideas and therefore greater competition in the affected and created industries. For if neither the inventor nor an interested manufacturer has to face the uncertainty of a negotiated per-product rate and the possibility of being refused on the basis of their negotiating positions, the product can be successfully produced by a number of competitive manufacturers. The only flaw in this arrangement is the lack of a transition from introduction to being put in the public domain. In fact, there is an incentive currently for manufacturers to wait out the time limit for patents and copyrights so that they can produce salable goods, license-free. It would then seem to be more reasonable to establish licenses at declining rates after the total licenses purchased have reached certain thresholds.

Once the rate has gone to zero, the patent or copyright will have entered the public domain, the inventor or author having reached a reasonable lifetime reward for their discovery or writing. Companies wishing to add a product to their line can procure licensing at the same or lower fixed rates then before, thus easing entry into its market. Successful inventions would thus be widely used by a number of competing firms. This then helps to establish their use so that production can continue well beyond the expiration of the license rights under the patent. With this wider adoption of ideas and this more certain reward for authors and inventors for their advances in the arts and sciences, popular capitalism more fully implements the patent and copyright clause of the Constitution.

The second objective is to restore invention to its proper locus: the community where the inventors and authors live. Popular capitalism achieves this by freeing creative minds from the necessity of earning a living outside the home. Instead, authors and inventors earn what money they need for supplies either through the returns from past efforts or through whatever tasks they can perform that will pay for those supplies with the fewest distractions from their creative efforts. With plenty of household chores, for which the college would rather pay at a reasonable rate than relying on the good graces of a few members, the stereotypical waitresses, waiters, cooks and cleaners looking for their big break can do so at home. Opportunities would also exist in college shops serving their neighborhood and in public service in their ward, though with a little less freedom. Once these supplies are purchased, they can be used in the studios, laboratories and artisan spaces which would be available in their college. Art and writing can be sold in the college shops. Prototypes can be tested on their college farm, in its artisan spaces or in its laboratories. By allowing inventors and authors to stay home with space for living and working, with opportunities for earning money for supplies and equipment and with avenues for selling their works and testing out their inventions on a small scale, popular capitalism returns the locus of invention to the home from its long exile in distant corporate fiefdoms. At the same time, efficient production returns to the company, now humbled to do the bidding of the colleges and the marketplace.

The third objective would be to restore the locus of the education which forms the basis of such invention to the same locale. Indeed, the Latin name for the style of household which we have been advocating, *collegium*, is the same as is used for our current institutions of higher learning: *college*. Another bit of Latin, the phrase *alma mater*, emphasizes the maternal role played by this home for learning. So it should not be any surprise that a home can be a school, nor that traditionally the school was in the home. Certainly, it will be a great relief to parents to not send their children prematurely into the world, and to what end? To learn material which is less difficult to comprehend than that in most of the books in the family library? To satisfy some nebulous, hidden and shifting criteria for being a grade X reader? This is madness! Parents have every reason to be nervous sending their children to school.

To the parents' objections, the educational gurus proffer the much ballyhooed *socialization* of the public elementary school, but that is better achieved among one's close friends and neighbors living together in a neighborhood or, in our model, a college. Indeed, how many times have we, as parents, seen the best friends of our children in the neighborhood become also their best friends in school? So this *advantage* of the public schools is as parasitic as it is unnecessary. Moreover, the learning of the dining table, of the book store or library event, of the lyceum of times past — which is restored in the lectures held in the college theater — and of nature and history walks, these all provide social learning for all ages and thus the most complete socialization. Public school socialization, with its peer gangs and cliques, is a poor and dangerous alternative.

With the education of children returned to their homes and colleges, the public schools can be put to better use in the training of civil servants, such as doctors, precision machinists and engineers, for work in government or in the capitalist industry which helps pay for that government and rewards the colleges which invest, continually, in it. Their laboratory facilities can be rented out to the public, augmenting those in the colleges, or to be used by medical researchers hired by local government. School district offices can be used as local offices of copyrights and patents, staffed with workers who are qualified to review the applications, particularly of new medicines. The classrooms can also be used in the teaching of various upper-level courses in which the public requests instruction, either to help them pass a course examination or for general interest. The meeting rooms and auditoriums can provide a forum for researchers, teachers and other interested parties, and further the restoration of the lyceum speaking circuit. The only elementary education which can reasonably be continued is the one which inspired its creation: the education of immigrants in the civic language, responsibilities and rights. The proper place for this education would be in the immigrant houses where it can be expanded to the adults. Once we are, in the provision of the necessities, actually welcoming our recent immigrants, instead of exploiting them, we may find that their adults have a greater hunger for schooling than their children.

These reflections on the transformations which might follow the establishment of colleges and villages, and their role in the maintenance of popular capital, lead us naturally to the construction of the *polis* at its first and higher levels. The style of construction, similar to that of colleges being built from families, we shall call *urban federalism*. The underlying principle is to build on what has already been established, to preserve the sustainable prosperity of the lower levels. Having eliminated poverty in the *oikos*, we do not want to introduce it again in the *polis*.

Urban Federalism

Thus far, the objectives and reforms we have set out could be fully implemented in a self-contained, sustainable village of colleges. As we have previously pointed out, the colleges are self-contained and sustainable in an ecological sense, themselves households and ecosystems in one. Then, by issuing currency and distributing it weekly to its people, the village gives them the power to choose which of these sustainable communities to join and, week by week, to remain, until it becomes progressively less a conscious decision and resembles more a natural desire. In effect, the provision allows people to choose where and with whom they will live, making these intimate choices out of love, rather than necessity. For the home is built on love, as is its cognate, domain. The reason for our Work is Love and not the other way around.

It was pointed out before that a family does not turn out its infirm or abandon its children or parents. This is not from a calculation of their projected worth or from an expectation of inheritance. If that were so, we would be repulsed, as we are, by the behavior which comes from such calculations: macabre fights by heirs or inconvenient babies thrown out with the trash. There is no reason to not be repulsed by less outlandish acts based on the same calculations. It is the replacement of affection with a cold calculation of impersonal benefits that is extremely offensive. Sentimentality is valid in this case, for it is by our sentiment that we react to all lapses of care, being an honest response of our hearts, so that more extreme cases merit more extreme sentiment. The extremity of our reactions is invalidly dismissed with the cavalier assumptions embedded in a word, as if there was no cause, as if the reaction came out of the blue. There is no look for a cause, nor yet again at its extremity.

Yet the cause is there and the extremity is clear to anyone with a heart. Sending one's children away to stay with strangers for the prime hours of the day for a higher future income, by someone's calculations, is repulsive. Leaving one's bride to an empty home after, not a full honeymoon, but perhaps a honey week or fortnight, so that one can earn more money from a successful career is repulsive. Going off to work each day, leaving your home while your children are yet young, while wonder fills their eyes on every turn, and to miss this all for no good reason, but only to pay bills, is particularly repulsive.

In fact, fathers find this so repulsive that many will resist their wives doing the same and will not tell them the reason why, as it fills them with shame. Every father wants to be able to stay at home, to enjoy his family, to play with his wife and his children, to work together in keeping their home tidy and in performing, as a family, the necessary chores of their community. To be unable to do this, to have instead to go outside of the home to work under a boss, in a servile and demeaning capacity, is a mark of failure, and having his wife also go to work, under like circumstances, merely compounds his failure, his shame at being sucked into the world of wage slavery. On finding themselves there, what mother or father has not looked around and asked: "What am I doing here? I gave up eight or more hours with people who adore me, to be with people who never miss an opportunity to bring me down in the attempt to bring themselves up and to be ordered or cajoled by that special brand of tyrant, the boss, to spend even more of my time away from my family." The answer is always the same: "The money", to which is wistfully added by some: "The vacation days and retirement." Translation: "I am giving up my family time because, by some cold calculation, our finances will be better and, possibly, we might be able to enjoy some brief interludes where my spouse and children are all awake and not miserable in an automobile getting to our vacation spot, all before returning to a home which all my children left some years ago with maybe my spouse to greet me." That is not a cheery picture, Ebeneezer!

The provision, by removing the repulsive notion of *working for a living*, frees the people to follow their hearts, joining into couples, then families and colleges. Each is more stable than our comparable residences. Freed from the stress of employment, couples can stay together for the decades of their lives. Over centuries, as generations past fade into memory and descendents of those generations become more distant cousins, there may be an evolution of the family, but no real break in continuity as the family remains in their apartment. Half the children of each generation will move out to join their spouse in another apartment, their children living with an extended family other than the one with which they grew up, but half will remain and bring their spouses to join their family, preserving its continuity and its stability.[1] An adventurous few may even move out of the college of their birth for their marriage but, with well over five hundred potential spouses of their generation and the gender they desire in a college of about 4200 people, those will be very few indeed. If an average of twenty chose a partner outside their college,

---

1 Some parents and grandparents of the moving spouse may join that college, as well, to be with their grandchildren and great-grandchildren. Particularly if they are sojourners or immigrants, there may be a blending of their family with the college itself, a wedding often being an occasion for romance to bloom among the unmarried and, to each other, exotic guests. The remainder of that family could be welcomed into the college as guests of honor, staying in the guest lodge, or as friends of other college families, staying in their apartments. Alternatively, if there is a vacant apartment, resulting from mergers of dwindling college families, the entire family of the moving spouse, possibly with the newly married couple, could take up residence there.

and half of those chose to join the partner's college, then those would amount to only one percent of their generation from their college. This practically assures that a set of families can reside in a college indefinitely. When no person needs a job or, more precisely, wages from a job, and the thought of leaving their home to get just any job becomes too absurd to be contemplated, then the social continuity and stability of each college is nearly certain.

A college having great stability in its residence is then assured that its stewardship will be rewarded. This brings the willingness of the college members to engage fully in that stewardship: composting its waste collecting energy from the elements at hand, and thus forming the regular patterns of life by which a college becomes sustainable. The ecological sustainability of a college is thus made possible by its social sustainability, which is enabled by the provision of the necessities, which its village engineers with a closed-loop currency, thereby avoiding dependence on anything from outside the village: socially, ecologically or financially.

It is therefore not to fulfill some essential need,

some requirement of life, that the village would view its relations with the outside world. Beyond the necessities directly furnished by the college, the niceties of life would be offered by the college itself, the home shops and the college shops on the street. These also would offer some necessities produced with less expense and effort by the village companies. What remains to be sought beyond the village resembles what is offered beyond the necessities directly furnished by the college: niceties not available within the village and goods offered at lower prices than are found in the village. One might dismiss this as a mere marginal saving, but from such marginal saving comes the scope and power of the free market, here in the form of free trade.

Indeed, this would be free trade in its fullest and purest form. There is nothing in this objective of external policy to suggest co-dependency and therefore nothing that would justify conquest or imperialism. For if there were a mutual dependence, there would be an incentive for one of co-dependent communities to satisfy their needs through conquest, rather than trade, denying the others the satisfaction of their needs through imperialism. Therefore, the village, free of co-dependency with any other community, has no need for conquest, imperialism or *global competition*, and no need for interdependent external relations.

Rather, the external relations of villages should preserve their independence while enhancing the quality of life for their people. We might call this a *co-independent* relationship when applied to two villages and an inter-independent relationship for more than two, but there is a less awkward and more familiar word to use: *federalism*. This word suggests the natural way to establish those relations, namely by building larger independent entities out of smaller independent entities. Since we are starting with villages and building the next larger entity, a city, we shall call this kind of external relations policy: urban federalism.

Yet we have already started this process in building up the college and then the village. We have already presented, in some detail, the finished product of that process in the college and the village, but it would be instructive to imagine how it might reach that stage. Since the glue of federalism is trade, we will look first at the family businesses and how the stores and studios which currently house them would be best converted into a suitable architecture for the college. The outward-facing family business would, of course, be the most familiar and accessible to the external observer. Most of these are in buildings separate from any residence; only the family members running these enterprises provide a clue to their familial associations. If the neighborhood is the college in formation, we can well envision another family in that college owning and operating the store or studio in that location.

Some of the stores and studios, however, will be of a piece with the residences of the families running the businesses at those locations, so that they will not be suitable for common use, even for leasing to other college members. Rather than trying to work around or legislate against them, as the zoning laws do, we should embrace these arrangements as an object lesson of what is required for a family dwelling in college architecture. That is, each family should have at least one exterior room from which to conduct business with other college members. The intimacy of this business and of its location requires that both the admission of any outside clientele and the regulation of its practices be decided by the college. Such businesses are analogous to the businesses in apartment buildings or hotels which serve their residents and visitors. As the benefit of these services is solely for these residents and visitors, so also is the cost. Thus, any pollution or nuisance created by these businesses would be solely the concern of those same residents and visitors. The college regulations are therefore the appropriate means to address such concerns rather than zoning laws from more remote governments. This example thus demonstrates a general principle of federalism: the federal concern extends only to the public space of the constituents.

There are other lessons to be drawn from this nascent federalism of the college. Chief among these is that the financial independence of individual, mature citizens, along with the ultimate financial dependence upon them of governments at each federal level above them, is essential to the democratic functioning of those governments. If anyone feels that they need to reside in an apartment with a group of people because of poverty rather than from familial love, they will silence their own voice out of that necessity and the people will not be heard. If a college manager can hire outside help with his own money, he will not heed the college membership. Thus, we assure democracy by dividing each provision payment equally between the individual, their intimate family, their extended family and their college, by making companies at every level dependent upon the regular investments by members at that level and by making the government of each *polis* dependent on the revenue accruing from their implicit, *ex officio* investments in those companies. The office justifying their half of the revenue is not only or even primarily that deriving from the infrastructure which allows a company to function, but is fundamentally that deriving from the provision of the necessities to the people — as individuals, intimate families, extended families and colleges — which allows their goods and services to be bought, and their revenue to be generated. The entire operation of such federal political economies would ultimately be based upon their paying the cost of their sovereignty. Thus, each higher federal level of the *polis* would pay the provision to each individual, in its own currency, as well as operate currency exchange services which are accessible to the people. Note that this does not create a dependence upon the higher currencies, as the village currency will be used in the local shops and as the placeholder for the necessities which the college physically provides. Rather, the provision in the higher currencies will be automatically exchanged[1] for the local currencies in markets driven by trade.

The other lessons and principles are related to this chief one in that they preserve the financial independence of citizens and limit the power of each federal government over the governments below them. Thus, as public hallways and elevators do not run through apartments, where they would create a cost of inconvenience in personal movements, no thoroughfare for a higher federal level should be allowed to interrupt the more local, and less expensive, traffic at the next level down. This federal separation of traffic is

---

[1] Individuals may choose to override this automatic exchange, in whole or in part, for however long they deem fit, but only for their quarter of the provision and only if they have not already designated that portion taken in the federal currency to be automatically distributed to some other party. We can allow individuals this latitude for their own, personal speculation in currency, but not to force such speculation on others.

accomplished at the most intimate level by the walls of the apartment, so the traffic outside that border stops to enter securely at the door or gate. This then suggests a general principal of each part of a federation having its own wall, which traffic between them never crosses, but stops to let its passengers enter securely at the gate.

Similarly, the possession and control of any space and resources within those walls that are not within the walls of the next level down belong to constituent entities of the body politic enclosed by those walls. The public rooms are operated by and for those entities either as a whole or as a collection of entities authorized by the whole to both operate and fund their mutual enterprise. Within the family apartment and its intimacy, this authorization can be informal and applied to solitary operators: Grandfather tutoring students in the classics or Mother selling books and wind chimes. In the greater household, slightly less intimacy requires slightly more formality and more participants, as was described above in the college stores rented by college families investing a fixed portion of their provision every week. We have also had a glimpse of this principle in the joint stocks of village enterprises being owned by colleges in the village.

Taking this further up the federal chain, city enterprises can be operated and funded by the villages. At our topmost federal level here in the United States, the federal enterprises, as opposed to governance, can be operated and funded in a standard and systematic way by subscribing states. Note that there is no place in this scheme for private ownership of enterprises with a federal scope, and definitely not for federal governance. No private or foreign interloper is allowed to play that part, even in a college. The power of the people is thus defended from those who would insinuate their money into the people's political economy, widen the scope of their influence and then proclaim themselves necessary to the performance of any public act the people endorse. Such is the method of financiers who, of old, held kings and emperors in thrall. We will have none of that here because it is excluded by design.

This may also be viewed as the preservation of sovereignty in federalism. Such a perspective allows us to posit a synthesis of protectionism and free trade.

When considering trade in general, we recognize that the participants are individuals for that purpose, so we should also recognize that they are individuals for other economic purposes, especially for those affecting their capacity to trade of their own free will. The absence of any coercion, in turn, requires that they first protect their sovereign selves, their individuality. For this more general view of trade, then, an individual in a couple is, of course, an individual citizen, but an individual in an extended family is a couple, an individual in a college is an extended family, an individual in a village is a college, an individual in a city is a village, an individual in a county is a city, an individual in a state is a county and an individual in a country is a state. These federal individuals all hold as their domain their own sovereign possessions in industry as well as in those things most intimate to them. In this regard, it is the friendship, affair or marriage, as a thing, which is possessed by a couple, never the people involved; such a possession is never owned without the risk of losing it altogether. So also are the ties of kinship within an extended family, the fellowship within a college, the civility within a village and the comity among the members of higher federal unions, integral to their respective domains. Even the thought of trading in these is an act of betrayal akin to high treason. Moreover, it is only when those bonds of affection are assured that a federal entity can trade at all, for, without them, the trade is not between that entity and another, but between some unfaithful member and an alien interest. Finally, for the trades of an entity to be freely entered into, the survival of all its members must be assured, so that its physical heritage is not made into property and traded desperately away. In the context of protection and free trade, we protect our domain so that we can freely trade mere property.

The possession of industry is no less an integral part of the domain of an individual of any federal level, and therefore a key to sovereignty. It should be clear that individual citizens have a sovereign right to their industry, which we call *labor*. Throughout history, lack of that sovereign right made you a *slave*, not a *citizen*. Landed property, not to be confused with a domain, has been considered a basic requirement for citizenship. Yet landless people are still considered citizens and, in our major cities, the most prominent citizens are landless, renting luxury apartments. The primary sovereignty of individuals is over their own industry.[1] Under popular capitalism, that sovereignty is assured by the provision of the necessities, so that sovereign industry is never traded away under duress. Individual citizens may offer their civil service to institutions or government, or work for their own ends. Individuals never sell their industry, though they may trade the products which come of it.

Now the college is the federal level at which individual possessions are first held in land as well as industry. This is because the college is the culmination of the *oikos* as a self-sufficient yet intimate community. As such, it becomes a fitting steward of the land held in domain at its atomic basis, a building block from which other domains in land are constructed, while preserving its own integrity and self-sufficiency. The village then preserves the land domains of the colleges, including

---

[1] This is what makes wage slavery, and the blasé attitude toward it, so distressing, so dissonant with our supposed freedom in this country. The labor unions, which arose out of the ill effects of wage slavery, do not contest wage slavery itself but, instead, revel in it, undoubtedly because people, once enslaved, once inured to being treated like cattle, are more inclined to take on new masters, especially those claiming that there will be better pasture and more commodious barns under their ownership. For these benefits the union bosses then demand fealty.

them inviolate and intact[1], while adding connecting and surrounding land for the welfare of its member colleges. At each level, a land domain is protected by its holder as an individual for the welfare of its membership as a federal union. Thus, for land, as for industry, for heritage and for intimacy, what defines an individual entity must be protected, lest it lose its identity.

It is then those things which do not define us, which we could get from there as well as from here, that become articles of trade. Such items are valuable, still, without being wrapped up in our identity prior to our acquiring them. We may even make them our own, part of our style, once they are in our possession, but until we trade for them and have them in hand, they are just one of some quantity of like things for sale, whose

---

[1] Hence, the principle of *eminent domain* conflicts with federalist construction. In federalism, no domain is *eminent* over others, so *eminent domain* has no place in a federal entity, even with *just compensation*. Its inclusion in the U. S. Constitution is a vestige of the then-current theories of *natural law*, which had many royalist proponents, and the flat federalism of the day, which viewed the states as sovereign powers whose internal organization was only required to be *republican*, not *federal*. We inherit this flat federalism in our assertion of *states' rights* without any mention of *counties' rights* or *towns' rights*. This is where *urban federalism* radically deepens federalist concepts in rejecting the application of *eminent domain* by the states and its vestiges in the U. S. Constitution.

value is based on their similarity to other articles being supplied to meet the demand from others like ourselves. That precious stuffed toy to which a child gives their own pet name, was once just one of a horde of similar stuffed toys coming off the assembly line. So also, with lesser or greater sameness, are the works of art from a famous artist that are commissioned by cities or bought by them in the after-market. The sameness is seen by the works being referred to by the artist's name rather than by their distinctive character. If a sculpture is still referred to as *The Moore*, *The Picasso*, *The Rodin* or *The Saint-Gaudens*, it might as well have remained on the auction block. There it will fetch a hefty price, but as soon as it becomes a part of our identity, it becomes priceless and thus beyond the reach of trade.

So regardless of whether the things we buy in trade become invested with our identity or are simply practical implements of our life and work, our welfare is improved by our purchase if the cost to our welfare is not better than the benefit we derive from them. This is necessarily a highly individual assessment and so is best effected by the individual choice to buy certain things at the offered prices and to not buy other things at their offered prices. In effect, each individual is placing bids on an array of trade items and trading when the offer price is less than or equal to their silent bid. The prices, themselves, have meaning only in this give-and-take of the market participants and in the context of the market in which they are participating. The currency of note is therefore the currency of the market and, this being a federal market, the prices are expressed in terms of a federal currency. Yet that federal currency has, in its first instance, no intrinsic value, being a flow of funds from the village to the people, to the companies and institutions they patronize and back to the village. At higher levels, the people may never see the federal currency, since it is converted into their local village currencies as a matter of course. The mystery of this conversion is solved and the purpose of the federal currency is made plain in the federal market, where it is the medium of exchange between the member goods and currencies. In other words, the meaning of prices on the federal market is to coordinate the price structures of the individual members so each sees in simpler terms the comparative advantage of buying some quantities of certain goods, rather than making the goods themselves. Thus, the individual members of a federal union can best arrange their resources and efforts for improving their individual welfare if each freely trades their export products and individual currencies as members, while preserving and protecting their own individual, sovereign interests. Thus, in our federal model, the *self* in Adam Smith's *self-love*[1] is itself a federation and his observation gains a wider meaning and application.

The converse, where the walls of sovereignty and thus federal identity are torn down so that goods can be shoved down the throats of local economies, comes at a cost. If it was to the benefit of the Japanese or Chinese people to *open up* trade with the Western World, it could have easily been accomplished with tourists and smugglers. The expense of a military foray

---

[1] "But man has almost constant occasion for the help of his brethren, and it is in vain for him to expect it from their benevolence only. He will be more likely to prevail if he can interest their **self-love** in his favour, and shew them that it is for their own advantage to do for him what he requires of them." "It is not from the benevolence of the butcher, the brewer, or the baker, that we expect our dinner, but from their regard for their own interest. We address ourselves, not to their humanity but to their **self-love**, and never talk to them of our own necessities but of their advantages." (emphasis added) [SMITH], pg. 14

shows that something other than the mutual benefit of trade was at play. Specifically, mercantile interests were seeking an imbalanced trade across the whole spectrum of goods rather than allow some of the industries, those of comparative disadvantage, to *fail* in the West, as was incorrectly, and probably not sincerely, supposed to be the consequence of free and balanced trade. The truth is that a few monopolists sought an unfair advantage with the assistance of their governments.

Similar motives, if not methods, are deployed internally against the local economies in the United States. The people bear the huge cost of the automobile in highway construction and maintenance through their taxes and in the operation, maintenance and storage of their automobiles more directly, not to mention having children and the elderly maimed or killed by motorists intruding on their walking and living space, all so that they can have products sold to them without them being given the chance to sell any of their products in return. What was once accomplished with gunboat diplomacy is now more civilly and insidiously achieved with motor roads, driveways and parking. In many cases, civility is dispensed with, as the commercial structure of villages is attacked and their venerable merchant buildings and elegant homes, which testify to their once independent and robust commerce, demolished over the objections of the few remaining and stalwart defenders of the local realm. This is all done for an alleged benefit of saving a few pennies for American consumers and renters, who now have gained a better appreciation of the one-way commerce and accompanying propaganda their Asian counterparts went through more than a century ago, when they were told by the gunboats that they had to be, in our modern phraseology, *globally competitive*. With their local industry, business and employment lost to state, national and, now, global firms, that appreciation is probably the only thing any American citizen gains from this domestic imperialism.

Returning to the positive case, another federal principle we can see from the collegial household is in the two types of interests involved: the individual and the familial. Both interests need to be represented in governing that college: the individuals to ensure that rules governing its operations are generally acceptable to its residents, the families to ensure a fair and stable application of those rules to their joint, communal life. Thus, individuals would be the creators of any rules for their college, with the families in a senatorial role, moderating any excesses. The rules of the village are applied less intimately, applying only to interactions on the street. The stability and fairness of these rules then becomes a concern of the colleges as the constituent parts of the village. With their old role moving up one level, the families then become the creators of rules. Yet, individuals retain their authority over the operation of rules at every level by electing the person responsible for that operation. This election, however, then poses a new problem, of large families casting more votes than small families, so that an executive favorable to small families might never be considered. The solution to this is to vest the nominating power in extended families, as well as the intimate families, and have the executive elected from a small field of nominees by a popular vote. In general, the principle is that legislators represent the members of the next federal level down, that their laws are approved by representatives of the members of the current level and that the executive is popularly elected from a short list of candidates nominated by a general assembly of representatives both of members of the current federal level and of members of the next federal level down.

This principal should be applied at every level of federation and is seen in part in the United States Constitution, before the popular election of Senators, with the Senators representing the interest of the States and appointed by the State governments, with election of Representatives from districts roughly corresponding to counties, and with the Electoral College using those same districts to elect the President. This is not an exact correspondence, but suggests reforms that can be made at the federal level to more closely align our electoral process with this federal process, so that the people can preserve their power in their more local government. Specifically, a constitutional amendment can replace the party conventions with a Nominator College which meets in the District of Columbia to pick the first field of five candidates acceptable to 95% of the nominators, set the boundaries of the congressional and nominator districts to be those of the current counties of the states, restore the selection of Senators and State nominators to State governments, and elect the President by popular ballot, the choice being among the nominees selected by the Nominator College. The Vice-President would be the runner-up in that election, as was the case before the Twelfth Amendment was enacted, that amendment being repealed. Giving that office ombudsman duties, as well as the appointment to the Supreme Court of one justice per year, the justices serving in a rotation of nine-year terms, would then enhance the satisfaction of the people with the operation of the federal government. Not only do those in the minority have an advocate in the executive branch, but in the judicial branch, as well. Similar reforms can be implemented at further levels down, so that the counties, or parishes, form the state senate districts, the townships, or cities, form the county senate districts, and the villages, as presented here, form the township or city alderman districts.

In the middle of this federalist structure, we can introduce a slight relaxation to avoid some of the cost of maintaining walls and formal governments. Municipalities have intuitively recognized the need for this relaxation by creating wards or other political and administrative subdivisions whose boundaries do not interrupt the flow of residents around their borough or city. In our structure, the neighborhoods of colleges is the level at which we relax the federal requirements, because of the large number of families in its colleges and in its sojourner inn. Thus a ward of twenty-seven colleges and one sojourner inn, each with 96 families, would have 2688 legislators. Clearly, a strict federalism for a ward would stretch even democracy by petition and referendum about as far as it could be stretched. Also, there is no reason to impose a strict federalism on districts which straddle the line between the *oikos* and the *polis*. The wards can then be more properly viewed as the formation of the actual federal structure from its proto-federalist components in the colleges. A village of twenty-seven wards would then have a government consisting of a lower house of 756 college or sojourner inn representatives and an upper house of twenty-seven alderman. This formal *polis* of the village is then better suited than the wards themselves to manage the streets and utilities which connect their colleges, along with government and institutional facilities, within what is more a boundary than a border. Indeed, with the streets and utilities crossing those purely representational boundaries, and government and institutional facilities along them, the village will already have to administer portions of the street and utility network which are not clearly separated from what might otherwise be under the control of the wards. In this practical sense as well, the ward allows a transition from the *oikos* to the *polis* without awkwardly imposing an actual federal structure in the *polis* on a quasi-federal structure in the *oikos*.

This does not mean that there should be no character to the ward, that the colleges, families and individuals in the village are all in one large pot of soup and their representation by alderman is a mere and arbitrary formality, like congressional districts. Rather, the employment in the government facilities within a ward should be limited to citizens residing in that ward. That restriction has more significance than a cursory reading would indicate. Consider the effect of a police force on a neighborhood when comprised of residents compared to the effect when many of the officers come from other neighborhoods or even outside the city. One can simply ask why there are neighborhood watches and community patrols in a city or village with a police department, to see that the latter has the character of an occupying force when it does not employ all of its officers from within the community.

Less severely, we can think of our local librarian or curator and realize that they brought local color to their library or museum. These local civil servants are crucial to the identity of a ward because they help to define its boundaries in our hearts and minds at a very early age. We live on Patrolman Bob's beat, read books in Miss Purdy's library, learn about life in colonial days at Mr. Lee's museum and Dr. Gilbert calls on us when we have a fever. Then we see them at the butcher shop, the bakery, the florist and the baseball game. We shop, we play, we talk, we pray, we laugh, we cry with them. We congratulate them at weddings. We console them at funerals. We play with their children, their nephews and their nieces. We are part of each other and that makes us part of a community defined by their work. In this same way, some of the intimacy of the college extends into the wider world of the ward.

Nonetheless, as we move ever so slightly out of our immediate community of family and friends with whom we are eating and dwelling into that first level of the *polis*, the lesser intimacy creates needs which did not exist in the *oikos*. That is, the presence of people who are, relatively, strangers introduces an element of distrust which must then be addressed. Protection against attack becomes a concern, something which in all but the most severely broken families is unthinkable. The ease of sharing, the loose notions of property and the confidence in bartering dissipate once one leaves the front door. Also, in crossing that threshold, we meet other people with whose talents and skills we are not as familiar as with those of our college mates. As ward blends into ward to form a village, this intimacy further dissipates so that we have new needs to assure villagers of their safety from those outside their more immediate circle, to defend against what may be more real threats from outside the village or city, to create a currency in which villagers can have confidence in buying and selling amongst themselves and to certify the skills of prospective employees for work outside their college.

Urban Federalism

Yet, as with the nascent federalism of the *oikos*, neither the boundary federalism of the ward nor the true federalism of the village, city or broader political unions should trespass on the internal workings of their component units. Whenever such a trespass is allowed, the democratic authority which is closest to the people is separated from the component federal units, thus undermining the sovereignty of the federation. We see this breakdown of the legitimacy of local federations in our proverb, "you can't fight city hall". If your city did not interfere with the internal operation of your village, nor your village with the decisions of your ward, nor your ward with your college, nor your college with your family, you certainly could fight city hall in their limited federal concerns through your family, college, ward and village. The limit on these concerns under such an urban federalism would leave little if any need to "fight city hall" in the first place.

One of the most pernicious forms of trespass is when the exchange of goods for money is extended to the sale of land. Since land defines the domain of each college and the domain of each federal level above it, sovereignty and citizenship are both based on it. To sell one's land is thus to literally sell one's birthright of citizenship, and to borrow money to buy a home is to pawn that right so that it can be sold off to others. Yet, this is precisely what we have done in the United States, subjecting our democracy to the vagaries of debt. Before we can truly have an urban federalism, we must first end this market in citizenship. As with college membership, all moves into or out of a residence by a college should be accomplished by a rapid transfer, possibly of equity as with the Square Real Estate Deal suggested above, so that the unencumbered rule of a college over its land is never in question or, in the first place, established as the Square Real Estate Deal would establish the rule of the family over their home. Going forward, there should be no property in land.

The next most pernicious form of trespass of higher federal levels upon the lower is in the distortion of local markets through external debts and insurance on the sale of goods and services. This is seen in real estate, when bubbles burst and lenders are able to foreclose yet avoid any losses through federal insurance programs. However, the distortion appears in its purest form in consumer credit and health insurance. It is well to briefly review what that distortion is and the dangers it poses for urban federalism.

The offering of debt, the extension of credit, for a long term and applied to the purchase of goods inflates the prices of those goods by throwing more money at the same quantity of goods. This price inflation creates speculative opportunities for buyers and then investors to borrow, buy, sell and repay for a quick profit. Later buyers of the financed goods adopt the same speculative assumptions about the prices of these goods, namely that those prices can only go up. For a while, these assumptions hold true, the lenders seeing only interest payments, but no risk, in extending credit to new hires and even people with no real source of income except the expected profits from speculation. Eventually, though, that extension becomes too tenuous to be repaid by some of the newly hired who, in their novice status, became the newly fired when sales failed to justify their place on the payroll, losing their six figure income in the process. Then the new speculators find price increases slowing down enough to frustrate their attempts to turn a profit before the interest charges overwhelm them. Failure through bankruptcy and default then increases the supply of those goods, further deflating the prices, while the fixed value of the debt assures that the proceeds from the sale of the goods, even if retrievable in the bankruptcy, will not be enough to pay back the creditors. The loss of principal deprives other markets of money which the creditors would have otherwise spent, either directly with the proceeds from the sale of their investments or indirectly with available cash being used to replenish their investment portfolios. This then exacerbates the collapse in the price of goods. The prices soon decline so far that, even though debtors might be able to afford further payments, the value of the goods as implicit collateral is so far below the value financed that it pays to walk away from them, letting the lenders seize those goods in the complete default we call bankruptcy. This process may be more succinctly described as the collapse of the credit bubble as it applies to furniture, electronics and automobiles.

Health insurance has a similar inflationary effect

as consumer credit. In both cases, what people pay for receiving a good or service is a small fraction of what the seller or provider is paid by the lender or insurer. The equilibrium price for a patient with employer-provided health insurance with 80% coverage is one-fifth of the equilibrium price for their doctor. That is, doctors can charge five times what they did prior to health insurance without any effect on their patients' out-of-pocket expense. Unlike consumer credit, though, health insurance inflation never subsides as there is no corrective mechanism. Instead, on the demand side, premiums escalate along with the medical fees until employers have to make a stand at their bottom line. Employee contributions are introduced, *managed care* rationing is implemented and prices are haphazardly controlled so that further increases in the total premium payments made by employers are moderated if not limited. These ineffectual attempts to forestall the logic of the markets are hailed as valiance facing doom.

A more accurate description would be farce covering for piracy. While the demand side inflation is unchecked despite the mock battles with public policy, health insurance is solidifying its inflation on the supply side, assuring the corruption of medicine and rewarding its pirate friends with all of the booty they can extort out of the economy. The money pouring into medical service drives up the prices of everything purchased by providers, as well as giving occasion for lawyers to reach into *deep pockets* for their tort suits. The absurdly high medical fees are thus back-filled with those prices, which are actually just forms of ransom. Medical school tuition is a ransom to practice medicine; Medical equipment is held ransom by rental agreements and *certificates of need*; physician wealth is the ransom demanded by predatory malpractice suits. In all of this, medical fees are not reduced, so we tend to think of them as *costs*, no matter how absurd, and that misnomer then allows the most grievous kidnapping and the most vicious ransom demand of all, lately enacted into law: *Subscribe to health insurance or you will never see medical care again!*

The application to the purchase of residences is clear. The inevitable result of the mortgage loan is a speculative bubble in real estate which, when it bursts, results in the blight of widespread foreclosures, thanks in no small part to the continued escalation of medical prices to care for grandparents and children, and of employee contributions into the health insurance scam, all of which eats into any paycheck the family may still have during that depression. Insurance of the mortgage loans, by reducing the price in financial discipline required of house purchasers relative to the bids they can place with borrowed funds, inflate those already inflated bids, in much the same way as health insurance inflates the bids for medical services, thereby further inflating housing prices during a speculative bubble. When the bubble finally bursts, the insurance loans then protect lenders and their prices on the now foreclosed properties. The borrower may not be able to sell his house for half the purchase price, but the lender has a buyer of last resort with deeper pockets and fewer qualms about paying claims than health insurers. If a private loan insurer is overwhelmed by claims, they are declared *too big to fail*, the federal government steps in to bail them out with public funds, which is the people's money, and a *budget crisis* is declared. If the loan insurer is directly the federal government, the defaulted funds are restored with, again, the people's money and a *budget crisis*. Thus, only by becoming *bank-owned* through the beneficence of citizens, including those being foreclosed upon, and only if no liens have been placed on it, can a house be bought for its deflated and real price. In many cases, a desperate and depressed town will prevent that from happening by clinging to the hope of taxes which will never be paid until mortgage loans start a new real estate bubble.

By that time, a family of local citizens have already lost the residence which establishes their right to vote, to petition their governments and to run for elective office. In other words, the people in that family lose their citizenship as a result of their conventional mortgage loan and the insurance on it. This is therefore a calamity for not just the family foreclosed on, but for the people in all the other families in the neighborhood. Their neighbors are set adrift and can no longer come to their aid when they are in trouble or in need. They are told that another family might move into the foreclosed house when the market picks up again. This is small comfort because if some family does, when it does, there will be years before that family becomes as trusted a neighbor as the one which had been so unceremoniously turned out of doors, out of those very same doors.

So we are divided and conquered, at the mercy of forces beyond our reach, strangers in our own town and set at odds with our own purpose in joining that neighborhood as a family. Our children no longer play together. They and we lose track of old friends and our sense of community. We gain apathy in its stead, rarely voting never mind running for office. Is it any wonder? When our home community has been dismantled by housing debt and insurance, the call of country becomes hollow and remote.

There are other threats to our current neighborhoods, analogs to the colleges here imagined. These are attacks on the sovereignty of and the freedom in our homes. Among these would be the freedom from unwarranted intrusions into our residence, from any restriction of trade or commerce approved by family or college, from any drafting for service of members of a family or college and from any requirement for a college or its members to pay taxes or to purchase goods or services against their will. Each of these attacks negate the good will among and good fortune of participants that a federation at any level requires.

Instead, each federal entity would instead do well to build upon the constructive efforts of its component political units. The parents should be able to care for their children without interference from family law and without *protective services* kidnapping them. What the small communities and colleges have built require no state authority. Indeed, the assertion of authority through legalized marriage strikes at the roots of the family, cutting it down with the blade of divorce. The boundary of the law is at the college gate, far from the family door. People should be able to declare themselves families without opening their doors to home invasion by the state. The mother should be able to declare that she will guard the external interests of the baby in her womb without granting a warrant for her own arrest should a state agency happen to decide that her child-rearing is in the way of their programs or their objectives. No law should approve or disapprove of her choice of guardians, her marriage, the composition of her family or college, her parental skills or the parental skills of her mate or partner, because that power of approval destroys the intimate bonds of the family and the community which built them.

The neighborhood should also connect college residences so that no expense is incurred in getting from the entrance of one college to the entrance of another in the neighborhood. For example, any roads which might discourage walking while encouraging vehicular travel should not be introduced . Those that do exist should be converted to pedestrian streets where possible or dismantled where not. Judicial banks and exchanges should be operated by the village to create local markets for the use of the colleges there. The village should staff and arm a salaried militia to protect their borders, enforce the law of the street and to meet the village's obligations for a broader defense. There is no need for a separate police force which would prove antagonistic to the citizens of the village. The village should also maintain a fire house and hospital, also with paid staff, supplies, equipment and medicine, to treat emergencies not handled by the colleges themselves. All utilities and communications between the colleges in the village should be owned and operated by the village government and connected at the residence border. No village should be dependent on an outside agency for basic facilities. Some revenue can be earned through utility and communications charges, but the bulk of a village's revenue should be derived from its investment in the village corporations. Though placing these two words, *village* and *corporation*, next to each other flies in the face of the current prejudice, there are good reasons for doing so in the popular capitalist lexicon.

Corporations were originally, and in the eyes of the popular capitalist should return to being, companies chartered to serve the public. Since their form of organization and mode of operation clearly show that they are governments, they can only serve the public by having less power than the most local form of democratically elected government and by being run as a subservient form of government. They only have less power than their neighborhood's government when their scope of operation is no broader than their neighborhood, when their employees are all citizens of the neighborhood, when their charter and formation is approved by a majority vote of the citizens of their neighborhood and the number of people fundamentally dependent on them for their livelihood, that is their employees, come from a small portion of the total number of households of that neighborhood. They can only be run as a subservient form of government when their employees are all civil servants, duly qualified for any office they hold, paid at the standardized pay for their position, sworn to uphold all of the constitutions within whose jurisdiction they operate, including their own charter, when they are wholly owned by colleges in their neighborhood, and when no college holds more than a small percentage of the total stock. Note that these rules will end most of the abuses of the corporate privilege which have so plagued our political economy, such as conglomerates, outsourcing, environmental damage, corporate crime, underpaid workers and obscenely extravagant executive pay and perquisites. These reforms are also part and parcel of an urban federalism in that they limit control at each federal level to those matters which are of concern at that level.

Now, these locally chartered corporations would operate in facilities and land set aside by the village which chartered them. For each such corporation, access to freight transportation, utilities and waste treatment will all be established by the village in that charter and by its infrastructure. Thus, the village would hold authority over that infrastructure, which is to say the part which pertains to its federal level. At each higher level, the authority over resources on common lands, their distribution to federal members, their use by corporations at that level, and the handling of whatever waste is generated by that use, is held by the federal entity at that level. Each federal entity keeps to its own concerns.

Similarly, each federal entity would run a stock exchange for the trading by its members in shares of its corporations. This stock would be registered on that exchange, so that any member which has held a share for a time sufficient to show results of their investment, say seventy weeks, can offer that share for sale to other members. Until a share is sold, its price is considered to be zero. After the first sale, the price of that share is its last sale price, positive or negative. This accurately reflects the actual price of the individual shares because each share carries an obligation of regular investments and the company may or may not have enough revenue to reimburse those investments in a given week, so that the one trade is priced for the revenue for the week in which it was traded. A proper gauge of the share price would then be the average of the individual share prices since it not only incorporates the price of each share, but recognizes that the old share prices are still valid enough to keep them from being sold for profit if they are overpriced or being bought at a premium if they are underpriced. However, this pricing is only important within the federal market, to allow members to adjust their individual investment commitments.[1] Indeed, all federal markets are intended solely for their members.

The federal commodities market, the other major federal market, will be discussed in great detail in

---

[1] For our current, non-federal stock markets, it could be of great consequence. When multiplied by a dividend rate set with other interest rates, the average stock price thus calculated could set a required weekly dividend for the company and thus assure that company profits are properly distributed to the shareholders, rather than being horded by its executives in a play to increase the company's share price and their own prestige.

a later chapter. For now, we will only point out that, by preserving the individual control of resources within a federal members' borders, urban federalism limits raw material exports to the first federal level where they can be put to productive use. It would never make sense to ship those commodities to a fellow member simply to combine it with raw material local to the other member, since the argument can then be made to ship the other raw material in the opposite direction. What is needed, by both members, is the greater productive capabilities of their common federal union. Otherwise, if they are both capable of utilizing the raw material within their domain to make some intermediate or finished product, then its location within their domain establishes it as part of their identity, as of their comparative advantage.

In closing this discussion of urban federalism, it is fitting to describe something it was designed to avoid the need for: the military. For the art of war has no part in federalism, being wholly replaced by the art of trade. Yet, the highest level of federal union must contend with external powers of nationalism and empire, and so is required to maintain a protective force against them, even as it tries to lead those antagonistic powers down the path of peaceful, loving federalism instead. Such a force would utilize the strengths of federalism: self-sufficiency and constructive enhancement. Thus, each village has a militia, which is the first building block upon which the military is built, by successive federal levels. The arms appropriate to each level will be made by manufacturing companies at that level which, as has just been described, are owned by the members of federal unions at that level. Then when the call is made from the highest level, an army of the people, supported by the villages on up, is ready to defend the highest level of their federal union.

For the next chapter, we return to the financial sphere in discussing the bank and exchange which will have a pivotal role in a full implementation of popular capitalism. This discussion, though, will be cast in a transitional or reform setting. As with any new idea, *popular capitalism* is unlikely to appear fully formed. It may, by its evolution, perfect its final form.

The Bank and Exchange

The Bank and Exchange

Perhaps it is most fitting that the Bank, which is emblematic of the financial authority of any State, is the institution through which we would implement the provision which establishes that authority. It is also fitting that such an institution, in performing that fundamentally constitutional function, should be run by the courts. This Bank would thus be a *judicial bank*, adjudicating financial contracts created by the legislature, as well as the social contract as a financial contract in the provision of the necessities. This fundamental purpose, at the heart of the authority and operation of a political economy, must rest entirely in the people's hands. Its operation should therefore be local[1], in the same way that the judicial system begins with local courts, and made to adhere to the financial laws of the people enacted at higher federal levels, with strict operational and civil service requirements set by the Supreme Court. The appeals process can be made part of the existing federal system.

The same requirements apply to exchanges, though the transitory nature of an exchange precludes against any appeals process. For the exchanges, federal structure is seen more in the scope of the market. Just as sisters do not exchange dresses or brothers toys through a global commodity market, so the participants on an exchange should be limited to members and treasury of the same federal union. Thus, colleges in a village

---

[1] This can be done in the United States most readily by using existing post offices, as advocated in the Populist Party platform of 1892 [HICKS.J.D.]. The current United States Postal Service should, however, be replaced with the judicial bank for its financial operations, subsuming the postal money order, and a Department of Postal Transportation and Communications to provide physical transportation and electronic communications not only for official government business, but for the needs of the people as well. Thus, another measure advocated in that platform, the government operation of the railroads, would be finally implemented. Needless to say, the corporation would be dissolved and all management and employees would become regular civil servants paid on the standard pay scale.

would exchange excess crops with each other and with the village. The village would buy from the colleges whatever is in greatest demand in the city exchange beyond its own supply and necessary reserves of seed and canned food. The Exchange, itself, would not own any commodities.

As a judicial bank, the Bank also would be barred from making any investments and taking any positions. The Bank and the Exchange would thus be prevented from causing panics or becoming embroiled in them. Market discipline can thus be maintained at all times since no matter which way the market goes, it still can operate because the market itself is not a player. Those who lose are allowed to lose no matter how big their failure and without raising questions which might undermine trust in the Bank, the Exchange and those most prevalent of contracts which connects them to the each level of the economy: money. Indeed, that trust comes from the very essence and meaning of money, which we will now discuss.

It should be clear to any appraiser of objects that the intrinsic value of our currency fails to approach its value in market. There is something besides the minting of coins or printing on fine paper that determines its worth. With the exception of a few economists, most people see it as the expectation that so much currency will purchase so much goods, an assessment which is only modestly altered each day. That is, it is trust. I might add, that it is this same trust that established gold as a precious, as opposed to a merely useful, metal. Trust in gold just has a longer tradition. Once people see how tacky it is and how limited its use, it will cease to be a source of monetary reform or even as a store of value. As the legend of Midas makes clear, a grain of wheat to a hungry man is worth more than a mountain of gold.

If we accept that trust forms the value in currency, we are drawn to the notion that it is in fact what we mean by money. This is confirmed when we assess our belongings. We expect things to be worth roughly what we paid for them, after depreciation. This trust is not totally blind, though. The relative prices of goods is based on bids which reflect the supply and demand of other goods. These relative prices are then cemented to the absolute prices by what holders of money gave away the day before and their willingness to give away something for money on the next.

For example, our willingness to work for a particular wage is based on the value we see in shops for that wage. If, after work, we find we cannot afford what we thought we could afford, we will be less inclined to work for that wage tomorrow. Together with our fellow workers in apathy and in looking for better-paying jobs, we will cause disarray in production that a savvy manager will notice. He will use that opportunity to bribe us with higher wages. If not so savvy, he will find shoddy products coming off the line and difficulty in replacing the workers who left. Either way, he gets less for each dollar spent on labor.

So we may define money as informed trust in values. In a currency-only monetary system, we find it calibrated by currency, that measurement being altered by the level of trust and the supply of currency. Thus, when new currency is printed and the same level of trust does not extend fully to the augmented supply of currency, then the money in currency goes down. When trust is lost and the supply of currency does not change, the money in currency will again go down. If we view each stock as a currency, we can see this effect of trust most dramatically on the stock market as a monetary system. As the mood swings from bullish to bearish and back again, the purchasing power of the stocks as a whole reacts accordingly, regardless of any change in the total number of shares.

The same effect is seen in banking as it operates today. Here, though, the trust is placed in borrowers to repay the loan with interest. When the general level of trust by banks increases, more money is lent. Though we may say that money is cheap, the case is really that debts are dear. Lenders fairly trip over themselves to offer the best price to any potential supplier of debt, in other words borrowers. When that trust declines, banks stop lending, except when they can get debt cheaply by lending to borrowers with no risk of default. Since such safety is found mostly in those with no need to borrow, there is effectively no market for debt; it has no value. If we want to revive the debt market, we must revive trust in actual borrowers. Giving more money to lenders will not help in the least.

It is questionable, however, whether investor confidence should be revived or money given to failed lenders in a private banking system. The success, even the survival of a banking company depends on it balancing the benefits of increased earnings from lending out depositors' money and the fatal cost of over-extension. To be sure, over-extension by a bank is discouraged in practice by the good sense of standards and regulations. However, it is a good sense informed by the loss of income from failed loans and eventually by the failure of the banking company. This is where reality intervenes, pulling the reins in on trust. Should the bank try to conceal their difficulties, prudent depositors may catch a whiff of the mounting defaults and pull their deposits. A more open bank may duly note its incompetence only to find depositors gradually shifting their funds to a competitor able to offer better rates. Either way, the overriding trust of the depositors in their bank enforces the discipline of sound lending if realty is allowed to intervene thereby.

However, if reality is not allowed to intervene,

then the extension of credit does not proceed on rational terms. The trust of depositors in their bank will then be misplaced. If the depositors do not pick up the tab from the defaults resulting from this breach of fiduciary duty, then they have no incentive to remove their deposits and discourage the poor lending policies of their bank. Instead, more and more money is wasted, eating into gains from good decisions and then into the bank's ability to handle even routine withdrawals. Other banks can be sucked in until a banking crisis is declared. Instead of there being a few stray bank failures and a small number of poorer but wiser depositors, a full-blown catastrophe is created where prudent depositors are made liable either directly in losing their deposits in a total collapse or indirectly through their association with the rescuer of the banking system. An objective observer unfamiliar with our system of banking would think it obvious that we shouldn't do that, but that is precisely what we do with our federal depository insurance.

To make matters worse, money lost for depositors and reimbursed by this blanket insurance increases account balances in private banks, precisely when trust in those accounts is virtually nil. With no money value for their accounts and when withdrawing cash may recover its value, there is a strong, rational incentive to keeping one's money in mattresses or at least working on a cash-only basis. This money is removed from investment, even if it is saved, in a more common and undocumented liquidity trap. We create a recession and to what end? Does it help people escape debt or poverty? Does it even fulfill the mission for which it was intended: to protect the savings of widows or orphans? No, its sole purpose is to force the people to underwrite the folly of bad lending from which they were never allowed to profit.

The new system abolishes this abuse of funds, this drain on the public wealth. It restores financial discipline to the marketplace and the adjudication of contracts and the operation of banks and exchanges to the courts, where these roles belong. The possibility of collapsing investment firms is hence nothing to be feared. The judicial banking system can proceed quite ably without them. Indeed, though the bank could either take them or leave them, the economy does much better without them. For as long as money is lent or otherwise speculatively invested, the prospect of investor failure is the only proper means of monetary control.

However, this reflection should make us question whether debts should be allowed at all. Once a judicial bank is established, the corresponding role of legislatures is to define the legitimate contracts and they could outlaw lending entirely. There is good reason for doing so. Debts are not only inflationary after a bailout, they are inflationary from the beginning. Money that would not have been available to bid on a product is made available by being lent to a bidder, thus increasing the winning bid and the price for that product. It is only when the loan is being repaid that any offsetting decrease in prices occurs and that on products other than the one bought with the loan, at later times than when the loan was made and only to the degree to which the loan is repaid and not simply replaced with other loans.

The uncertainty over whether the loan will be repaid, especially without being replaced with other indebtedness, increases with the term of the loan. This, combined with the diffusion of the products not being bid on and the smaller increments with which the buyer is withdrawing his purchasing power, assures that, for all intents and purposes, a long-term loan has negligible deflationary effect to counteract its direct and focused inflationary impact. Therefore, long-term loans should be expressly forbidden, as well as loans directed at any particular market or kind of product, whatever the term. Further, any loan which can easily become a *de facto* long-term loan should be prohibited. Thus, revolving debt on *credit card* or line-of-credit accounts should also be banned.

The only forms of debt which would avoid objection is commercial paper in its pristine condition, as a placeholder for secured and insured goods in transit and advances on certain payments in the near future, such as provision payments. These forms of short term debt increase liquidity in the markets without opening the door to speculation. That is, after all, the benefit by which most people justify debt in their own lives and which they extrapolate into the larger economy: lend-me-a-five-spot-until-Friday occasional financing. This is fine as long as the extrapolation is on the same kind of terms.

The money which the judicial bank handles is therefore of only one kind: currency. It may be in physically exchangeable form, as United States Notes in this country, or it may be a credit in the official account of a citizen. For the latter case, particularly in handling the provision, the judicial bank needs to have such an account for each citizen which is easily accessible to them in their village.[1] That accessibility also breeds trust in the ledger currency by the villagers. They know, by regular acquaintance, where their money is and how it changes hands. Similarly, a physical currency created by a village for the internal transactions of the village and, by and large, remaining there, would be well trusted by the villagers in the only period which matters for currency: the near term between when money is received and when it is spent.

It would certainly be more trusted by the local villagers than a remote currency, especially one tied to a

---
[1] Or in their apartments, as described above.

commodity and subject to the fluctuations of that commodity's supply and demand. To the hysterical rantings of the gold advocates, it should be noted in response that whether a form of money is trusted around the world by international traders is irrelevant to whether it will be trusted in our own village. We should not confuse the parties involved by imposing trade currencies on local economies. There are better ways of establishing trust in trade, as we will see.

Thus, the local judicial bank should only accept local currency for local contracts. This currency may take many forms, and could take more advanced ones as well, while remaining undeniably local. This allows local transactions and contract payments to be made with currency in the form of coins, paper, check, card and funds transfers, deposits and withdrawals through a teller or a computer of some kind. Limiting the local judicial bank to dealing with local currency for local transactions is not barbaric. Nor is it at all inconvenient. The Exchange is the proper place to conduct currency trading, because of the greater liquidity of its markets, and the local judicial bank would provide access to that.

The contraction and expansion of the monetary supply to match the cycles of planting and harvest, as proposed in the Sub-Treasury Plan, is no longer needed under Popular Capitalism. Instead of having a small and scattered population of farmers in our farming regions grow crops for the rest of the country and the world, we would have colleges growing crops for their much larger populations, with only the excess not needed for the survival and comfort of those larger populations being traded elsewhere. A good price for corn, wheat or cotton ceases to be required for the survival of the farm itself, so that good and bad prices for crops can be used for their proper economic purpose: to encourage planting of more crops in short supply and fewer crops in abundant supply. Moreover, the mixture of crops which a college would grow for their own survival, and the greater area devoted to that purpose than for a single-family farm, would discourage the ecologically and agriculturally dangerous practice of monoculture. Thus, agriculture would not be dependent on federal monetary policy. This allows a federal currency to serve its role as a trading currency, which we discuss next.

The Treasuries, Trade, Aid and War

The Treasuries, Trade, Aid and War

Having discussed, at length, the basis of an internal political economy, it is probably best to consider the place such a structure would hold in the greater world. Our more conservative friends claim defense against the allegedly hostile world beyond our borders as the sole legitimate purpose of government, while our more liberal brethren act on that basis once in power. Yet both American parties consider trade also within the purview of their policy platforms, an inconsistency justified by martial terms like *trade wars*. For both high purposes, the wealth of our federal treasury is instrumental, whether directly or insinuated by a strong dollar. A similar line of thought predominates in other mercantilist countries.

We have seen a different dynamic at work in our discussion of urban federalism which makes such a belligerent stance quite unnecessary. Certain features of federalism can be applied to world relations and trade to construct peaceful federal unions, even to encompass the globe. Before that task is complete, the military can follow the same federalist principle, established in our Constitution and then promptly ignored, of regulating and commanding the people's many militia by state and then federally, which we have revived here. We can then replace our race to the nuclear death with a gentler walk around the city walls. Perhaps this less ambitious, less grasping and more limited military will inspire our people and our leaders to also take a less aggressive stance on trade. Perhaps that less aggressive stance on trade will then make clear to those of greater pomp and power what the humble craftspeople and peddlers have known for ages: that there is more to be gained for all through trade than through plunder. Perhaps we might adopt that different cast of mind and seek prosperity for all rather than obsessively seeking dominion through growth. We can hope that the fruitful examples of cooperation through peaceful trade are persuasive.

The Treasuries, Trade, Aid and War

Still we must consider the possibility that trade is not given the chance to persuade. Let us then address directly the errors which are shrouding the benefits of trade and smash the false idols of growth and global competition. The plain truth is that growth has been masquerading as prosperity even as it undermines it. The people, being tricked by their governments out of the provision of the necessities, are thereby compelled to compete for servile jobs, just to survive. In order for jobs to be available to the mass of the people who, through this deception, now need them, the companies offering employment must maintain market share and, as companies in other countries compete for and win market share in older industries, the companies in a country losing market in one area must replace it with growth in another lest they lose jobs. Thus is born an obsession with growth and global competition, filled with horrific demands that children take on the stress of competing with their counterparts from halfway around the world in a reprise of the Children's Crusade, while the politicians chant their mantra of *jobs, jobs, jobs*. Out of this foolery, we are supposed to believe that perpetual growth will bring us prosperity.

Yet nothing can be further from the truth. Growth, as an end in itself, is antithetical to prosperity. For, in the end, prosperity makes growth unnecessary, while perpetual growth requires more unsated appetites, hungers never filled, so that prosperity never comes. The citizen under a policy of perpetual growth is thus a modern Sisyphus condemned to a nightmare of global competition, watching each hard-won victory being rolled down the hill, as a Sisyphus in another country pushes his boulder to the top of the hill after him. Each Sisyphus is cheered on by the political elite in his country with patriotic calls to push his rock harder and faster to the greater glory of his country. No mention is made of the greater profits of companies and financiers, which bear no allegiance to any country, except for a few of us who are so iconoclastic as to put the weal of the people above the patriotic shibboleths which exploit them. No mention is made either about the burden of private debt which adds greater weight to the Sisyphean boulder by increasing the demand for higher wages and thus for jobs, the competition for jobs leading to lower wages instead and then greater private debt. The chain to the boulder of jobs and growth is private debt.

Therefore, if the goal is prosperity and liberty for all, the lengthening chains of private debt must first be broken. This can be done by abolishing long-term private debt, after which further steps can be taken to secure freedom as suggested previously. Though greater prosperity should only be sought after securing liberty, that prosperity may itself bring economic independence and thus the liberty sought. In foreign relations, mutual prosperity may be enhanced by a peaceful trade based on a free exchange of goods for the mutual benefit of all of the trading partners. That mutual benefit comes from comparative advantage, as that concept was presented by David Ricardo.[1]

The internal concerns are easily put to rest by popular capitalism. Provision of the necessities moots

---

[1] [RICARDO], pp. 82-83. Mill wholly endorsed the concept and its associated policy of free trade, while conceding that other interests might take precedence over the economic goals of free trade. (See [MILL] pp.278-288.) George also wholly endorsed comparative advantage but recognized that the popular support of protection comes from a dependence on wages for survival. ([GEORGE FreeTrade] pp. 242-252.) Keynes saw some purely national benefits of protection for investment and employment, under the gold standard, thus limiting the practical application of comparative advantage without refuting it. (See [KEYNES GenTh] pp. 333-371) Indeed, Keynes endorsed a Free Trade Union as a post-war remedy equal to the League of Nations. (See [KEYNES EconConseq] pg. 266)

employment concerns, as the people no longer depend on wages for their survival. The end of debt money and legal support for long-term debt eliminates any role that might have remained for interest rates where wages are just the price of labor, investment is the commitment a college makes to an institution and profit is the result of deducting weekly investments from weekly revenues. There are no consequences to movements of economic values, save in the greater efficiency of the economy.

Popular capitalism goes even deeper. The great concern underlying all of protectionism, and anti-trade sentiment generally, is with the retention of that wealth which is deemed by a people to be their sacred trust. You will not find a New Yorker who would actually sell the Brooklyn Bridge, nor a bill in Congress to sell Lady Liberty. There are things, integral to our being, either as ourselves or as a community, controlled by us because we need them in order to physically be us, not only part of our personal and corporate selves, but our identity, as well, and our home. They constitute our domain and, for that reason, they are never traded, except as a form of suicide, from desperation or dissolution so complete that one would sell one's soul for a few short animal breaths taken in anonymity. In contrast, other things are merely products to be traded for other goods, which are then consumed in some sense. Such a distinction is implicit in Ricardo's examples, where the nationality of a worker makes them more productive in some trades than in others, their skills being part of the English or French domain. It is also in Mill's "greater interests than mere saving of labour"[1], the defense of the nation, or domain, being the only one accorded validity, and that only temporarily. In popular capitalism, this distinction brings a synthesis between protectionism and free trade: the domain, from the industry of the humblest person to the resources of the federal union, is protected by being excluded from external trade, so that its products can be freely traded.

Yet, many critics object to the notion that there can be peaceful trade. For their case, they can trot out a long history of mercantilist abuses of trade escalating to devices of war and conquest, which we will not deny have occurred and will continue to occur as long as

---

[1] See [MILL], pg. 281.

trade is conducted through a medium of exchange which is required to have some universal and often, toward that end, intrinsic value. Gold has often served that purpose, with the misery of oppression left in its wake. Currently, Debt serves this purpose more directly, the supposed credit-worthiness in seeking supposedly necessary new debt reducing once-sovereign countries to the humiliation of bankruptcy proceedings, with all of the attendant miseries of supervision by a receiver, dourly disapproving of every expenditure, however necessary and proper. Mercantilists will demand their pound of permanent and universal value for their transitory and specific transactions. Worse, they will inflict upon the people this universality of value in their most local and intimate transactions. Against this folly, the people have revolted at various times, demanding a supply of local currency sufficient for their local trade.

The critics then try to discredit this ready supply by sneering at it in high moralistic dudgeon, calling it *loose money,* as if the sovereign currency of the people was a cheap harlot. This is, of course, preposterous and reveals a fundamental misunderstanding of money and its different uses. If you were in a realm where the king decided that he would pay for your produce in dead pigeons, would you refuse him? I would think not, as he would also accept taxes paid in the same currency if he were reasonable. The dead pigeons would be the fiscal currency of your home country. There is nothing loose or cheap about it. Morality is irrelevant.

Now suppose you wish to trade with somebody in the next kingdom over, where the fiscal currency is in dead crows. Obviously, your pigeons mean as little to your trading partner as his crows mean to you. However, that does not mean that you should stuff pigeons down his throat or that you should be made to eat crow. All that is needed is for you and he to come up with a mutually agreeable trading currency. This trading currency does not need to be universal, nor should it be. As long as it works for the two of you, as long as there is a common bond of trust in exchanging your mutual trading currency with pigeons and crows, there should be no concern with what other people use with their trading partners. The key to a successful trading currency, then, is the partnership for which it is the seal.

Yet we have already a form of partnership in urban federalism. Each member of a federal union is a ready-made partner of the other members. Their federal currency is therefore their trading currency within their federal union and its member currency in the next federal level. For this formal trading partnership, there is no need for a universal currency as there is no need to meld their respective fiscal currencies into a common currency. The sovereignty of a federal union establishes the authority of its federal currency, without the need or tendency to reduce the sovereignty of any member or to diminish the authority of their respective currencies.

It is clear, then, that universal currencies are for casual trading partners. A traveler from a distant land, a smuggler, a pirate and a trader from a country which might be as easily at war as in commerce with your own, these all have a need for a universal currency like Gold or Debt. Rather than building trust, trading with gold is emblematic of distrust and trickery. The trading can be gamed. Want to get more of that precious olive oil without having to pay for it with goods produced from your own hard work? Just steal some gold from

The Treasuries, Trade, Aid and War

another country or continent and pay for the olive oil with that. Gold is gold, however it is gotten, and is therefore an easy way to cheat your trading partners.

With Debt, the tactics might be subtler and more refined, but the result is the same. By lending money to other countries[1], you are paying those countries money for a loan contract. That is, you are importing Debt. These payments going out must then be balanced against the payments coming in for your exports of goods. Your export industries flourish. Your workers are employed. You prosper as an *exporter country* as long as your trade is balanced with Debt. On the other hand, the countries which borrowed money from you are *importer countries* which cannot seem to get enough from their exported goods to pay for what they import from you. Their export industries decline if they ever develop. Their workers are unemployed. They fail as *importer countries* and, in that failure, are hard pressed to care for their burgeoning poor. Thus, instead of paying back the loans to reverse the trade imbalance in

---

[1] The money might also be lent to private concerns in the other countries, with the same effect. This backdoor to sovereign debt is another reason to abolish private long-term debt as well as alien ownership.

debt, they desperately seek more loans and remain *importer countries*. By use of Debt, you have cheated other countries out of the value of their real exports, have tricked them into financing your industrial expansion and have still been able to present yourself on the world stage as the epitome of financial rectitude. This deceit is accomplished with Debt, as well as with Gold, because any universal currency can be procured from outside of the exchange of real goods.

On the other hand, a federal trading currency, properly numbered and registered, is not gotten outside of the rules of exchange within that federation. Instead of a pirate's booty of gaudy gold, we buy golden saffron from one partner with the currency received for our olive oil sold to another. All are enriched, all made more prosperous by this honest trade. By the exclusion of Gold and Debt from the monetary system, the point of trade once again becomes an exchange of goods for the mutual benefit of all involved and not the futile acquisition of a universal currency either directly by hoarding gold or through a mercantile alchemy to transform loans into gold. We can therefore lay to rest all concerns about the *strength* of one currency over another and better credit ratings for unnecessary and, as far as trade is concerned, destructive debt. Trade is not some global competition, with winners and losers, but a cooperative effort where all are winners. This has to be the case because every trade is the discovery of a positive sum in the economic game. It is the business of the organization of trade and currencies to make that discovery easy and transparent.

This business is accomplished with the use of federal markets and currencies by bringing under one house the trade between the members and by providing a formal and objective mechanism for setting the value of each member currency in terms of the federal currency. Obviously, there will be individual trades by tourists and peddlers which will not be conducted directly at the federal market. Also, the sales of branded merchandise from the college shops, studios and farms are too varied in quality and kind to be sold in a formal market. The trade between member markets from these more entrepreneurial sources needs to be brought in through less direct means. It is therefore the direct trade in standard commodities produced by the bureaucratic companies owned by the members of a federal union, or by the bureaucracy of the federal union in agriculture or the extraction of resources in its specific domain, which forms the basis of its federal market and its discovery of the mutual gains from trade.

The input from tourists and peddlers can be incorporated into the federal market by currency exchanges operated by the federal government at every convenient location. Such federal currency exchanges would be freed from any need to operate at a profit, to bear the capital cost of unsold inventory or to suffer losses due to poor pricing. In short, these would not be businesses at all, but kiosks providing citizens a service of exchanging one form of money for another, at rates set at the last session of the federal market. A small fee could be charged per transaction to pay for the labor of the civil servants, but there would be no need for any spreads between the sale and purchase currency prices, such as are found at private exchanges.

Similarly, there will be a demand for currency in advance and, initially, for the repayment of old debts or obligations under cross-jurisdictional contracts which have not yet expired. Not only are these transactions unsuitable for kiosks, but there is less of a logistical need to limit the quantity of currency exchanged. Indeed, there are legal reasons not to limit the amounts required by old debts and cross-jurisdictional contracts, even though new such contracts would be forbidden on account of their making factors mobile or otherwise undermining the mutual advantages of trade. It should be noted that the daily requirements of any contracts being phased out and of any private or sovereign debt being gradually liquidated are themselves an upper limit on the quantity of currency exchanged and that exchanges in advance of a trip, as assistance to a friend, child or parent overseas and for similar purposes can be subject to individual and local daily limits. The amounts involved can therefore be prepared for, despite their larger size. Because of that size, which favors ledgers over physical handling of currency, because the net exchanges of currency will be smaller than their sum and because a judicial bank would have the knowledge needed to prepare for them, all of these transactions are best handled through the federal banking system described earlier. The net currency transactions can then be communicated to the exchange through orders to buy or sell the member currencies involved.

Similarly, the kiosks will replenish their stocks of some of the member currencies and dispose of their stocks of some of the others by entering, into the federal market, orders to buy or sell those member currencies. Stocks of the federal currency would be maintained by issuing or retiring previously issued federal currency rather than by placing orders. In all cases, movements of currencies, whether by orders or issuance, will be by block quantities of those currencies. The exchange can then treat currencies like commodities.

Next we consider the branded products, such as wine, cheese, preserves and custom crafts. Today's readers might well wonder why I omit corporate brands when those are currently the most recognizable. However, those same corporate brands are also the most easily counterfeited. Clearly, the products labeled with a corporate brand are not as unique as the corporations would have us believe. Mostly, they are manufactured products which are of a sufficiently standard form that they can and should be more efficiently produced by many competing firms in numerous locations. That is, they are more properly considered as commodities. This is why I limit consideration of brands to home and college based wares where the brand clearly indicates where and who crafted the product. A factory might can or package that product, but that is all they do; the label would be that of the craftspeople, which it is the duty of the cannery, bottling plant or packaging plant to verify.

All of this suggests that the federal governments should have an active role in the distribution of products to retailers, the better to maintain truth in labeling for the branded products. In fact, the increasing monopolization of retail distribution and its destructive effect on local economies, not to mention a history of oppressive rule by merchant companies, should have already convinced us that the fair distribution of products is a proper if not a crucial role of government. In this capacity, a federal distributor would collect orders from local shops for specialty goods offered at the artisan's price and converted at the current exchange rates. As with trade conducted by tourists and peddlers, the supply and demand of currency is the mechanism by which the trade in branded products is presented to a federal market.

This leaves unbranded goods, or commodities, including goods produced according to a patent license. Trade in these must not only be formal, with the quality of the commodities rigorously verified, but must also maintain sufficient reserves for domestic consumption, especially for agricultural and mining products[1]. Indeed,

---

[1] For agricultural products, the concern is with drought, as in the case of Joseph's interpretation of Pharaoh's dream. See Genesis 41:25-36 [BIBLE]. In the case of mining products, such as petroleum, the concern is with their eventual depletion. In either case, the reserves buy us time until resources can either be replenished or replaced. The time may also allow us to reconsider our earlier prejudices with regards to what is replenished and what is replaced. Our current mode of agricultural production may need to be replaced with one is which is more sustainable and capable of being used during droughts, say, by composting human waste and collecting waste water for use in roof top greenhouses and hydroponic gardens. Our supplies of metals and even of petroleum may need to be replenished through recycling and reclamation when new mining is no longer feasible or advisable. The failure to replenish will cause scarcity pricing to come into play, which the reserves will moderate while still encouraging replacement of the depleted resource or increased conservation of its use and eventual elimination of its demand. Toward the latter end, particularly with petroleum, the reserves of a resource are not sufficient to prevent calamity but require a scarcity tax on its more profligate uses, such as a gasoline tax applied at automobile filling stations, so that conversion to a pedestrian lifestyle, in this case, can eliminate demand for automobile fuel

these federal markets would be primarily commodity reserve exchanges. Toward this end, warehouse space should be reserved for blocks of these commodities, each sufficient to satisfy the weekly demand within a member[1], with enough block storage for an adequate reserve, say, 365 blocks for each commodity to cover a seven year reserve[2]. Each federal legislature would

---

    entirely and thereby relegate gasoline and its arguable substitutes to the occasional use befitting a precious commodity. This then returns us to the sustainable and intensive agriculture driven by horses and oxen having useful manure as a by-product instead of harmful air pollution.

1. We are only considering the demand of a lowest-level or "leaf" member here, because we seek a wide distribution of reserves. This is more appropriate for a federal system than a centralized reserve as Joseph had advised for the Egyptian Empire. Even as of this writing, large oil reserves are the strategic preserve of empire, giving excessive power to the higher-level federal government in the United States over the states, counties, cities and villages which are the source of those reserves, neglecting their demand while pursuing its imperial ambitions. Imagine, then, how power — literally — would devolve to the people if each village had its own prudent but non-strategic oil reserve of the same size as the oil reserves of each city, county, state and the federal government.

2. This arbitrary figure drawn from the story of Joseph has the advantage of being a historical account, albeit not up to modern standards, of a multiple year drought and the attempt to handle it with grain reserves. We provide greater security by storing seven years of reserves instead of the 1.75 years stored by Joseph., presumably sufficient due to a voluntary reduction in demand by the Egyptians and to the contributions, albeit meager, of a greatly diminished but not entirely absent yield. If we take the proportions as roughly indicative, then a seven-year reserve would be capable of handling a drought of 35 years, which is not unheard of in many parts of the world. Be that as it

Popular Capitalism

decide what commodities to list on its market. Members will select the commodities they will produce as well as consume, no producer of a commodity being exempt from its consumption. Every member will be committed to buy one block of each traded commodity per session, as long as they have not already reached their reserve capacity for that commodity. In order to ensure a ready supply of commodity blocks to be sold for each session, each member would have thirty-five additional blocks of storage available for each commodity they produce, so that they can accommodate seven weeks of five-day session without restocking. For the products they do not produce but wish to resell, this same amount of storage, thirty-five blocks, would be available. Altogether, each member would have allotted to it by the federal market, storage for 400 blocks of each commodity, of which 35 are *produce* and 365 are *reserve* blocks.

The federal distributors of branded goods would also distribute the unbranded commodities. Stocking of commodities produced in a member would start with federal distributors purchasing blocks of a commodity

---

may, a seven-year grain reserve far exceeds what is done currently and can be increased if deemed inadequate.

in those members where it is produced, at the lowest price they can negotiate. Some of these blocks will be held in the store, to fill local orders at commensurate prices, and some will be purchased at the same price for the member account at the exchange and placed in their *produce* storage, if it has not already been filled, at a rate of up to seven blocks of a commodity per session, depending upon how many *produce* block storage units remain empty. Each block retains the price negotiated by the federal distributor, in the currency of the member where it was bought. From there, it will be traded to other members, who will find it automatically placed in their *reserve* storage. The federal distributors for those members will then purchase the *reserve* blocks one per session, to stock their stores, there being none available locally at any price. The only prices are the trade prices of the *reserve* blocks, converted into the currencies of the other members. If blocks remain at the distributor by the next session, then the exchange account of that member buys them back at the same listed price. These blocks are then placed into the *produce* storage of that member, thus becoming a reseller. Therefore, once a commodity has been traded in the market for awhile, the members who are not producers become resellers as naturally as recyclers and used goods dealers serve a market after it has been populated with products.

Each of the federal distributors is an operation of immense size, as one might expect of a replacement for the large retailers of today. Besides a well-qualified staff, paid at the standard wages, each distributor would have a budget per market session equal to the average total provision of the villages within their jurisdiction, converted into the federal currency. For a single village, this would be nearly five billion base provision units. What needs to be kept in mind, though, is that the goal of the distributors is to buy the goods low and, when given the chance, sell them high. They are not given a chance when the exchange buys its goods for the price they paid, but they get that portion of the money back. All receipts go back to the federal budget at the level they serve, so the distributor could earn for its federal entity a small profit, as modest as it is free from all taint of gouging the customers or cheating the producers. More importantly, the distributors help establish a flow of commodities into the exchange. The exchanges also receive money from the participants for their purchases, but they also send money back to the participants for their sales. Here also, much money changes hands, but most of it flows through to be used in the next cycle.

The federal entity would also be a participant in the exchange at its federal level, with the same storage requirements as a member. However, the federal entity will acquire *produce* blocks in that exchange, while its *reserve* blocks will be bought in the exchange where it is a member, i.e. through external trade, if topmost, or else in the next higher-level federal market. As with its members, the federal entity would buy *produce* blocks also from the federal distributor at their level. The limit of buying at most seven *produce* blocks of a commodity per session applies to the total from both the exchange of its members and the distributor. The goal is to allow the federal entity to build up their *produce* blocks so that they can trade for *reserve* blocks, yet still compare the prices of the distributor with those of the exchange.

The corresponding limit on the distributor of purchasing only one block of a given commodity per session is based on its role of distributing commodities sufficient for one week for every person in the village, in that case, and of a similar flow for the higher federal levels. The expectation is that the distributor will skip buying some commodities in a market session because they are already stocked or they can find a better price locally. The flexibility which this gives the distributor allows it to better serve its customers through its better prices, while the ability of a member to access unused blocks prevents the needless stockpiling which might result from its abuse. This limit thus strikes a healthy balance between rationing and hoarding for distributors.

Returning to the federal entity, we note that at the top-level, a separate market for external trade needs to be established. This external market will require those seeking to participate to adhere to some essential features of the internal federal commodity reserve markets, namely that the commodities they sell should meet the standards established by the top-level federal union, that blocks of those commodities should be entered for sale at prices in their own currency and that, for any given session, they should be prepared to sell a block of their own currency for the trading currency at the price determined by the operation of the market. This may provide a transition from trade accords to peaceful federal union but, in what follows, we focus on the federal market of the members of a federal union. This not only simplifies the description of the operation of federal commodity reserve markets, but also makes for a cleaner exposition of comparative advantage in such a market.

We begin this more formal presentation by noting that each session of the federal commodity reserve market would move commodities from *produce* blocks to *reserve* blocks. To do this, each member would buy blocks of commodities for less than the price in their *produce* (as well as *reserve*) blocks or simply transfer their own blocks from *produce* to *reserve*. Orders from the distributor would then be filled mostly from *reserve* blocks as those would be at lower prices. Then the comparative advantages across the branded-unbranded divided are realized by setting the exchange rates of the member currencies with the federal trading currency in such a way that trade is balanced. By using a formulaic approach to setting the exchange rates and the transfer of commodity blocks, the process is more likely to be objective and hence more acceptable.

Thus, if n is the number of listed commodities, m the number of members in the federal union and b the maximum number of blocks of each commodity each member can hold for trade, then we can define:

$B_{i,j,k} \equiv$ the kth block of commodity i for member j
with $i \in [1,n], j \in [1,m]$ and $k \in [1,b]$

$B_{i,0,k} \equiv$ the kth block of commodity i for the federal entity with $i \in [1,n]$ and $k \in [1,b]$

It may happen that a member may not have k blocks of a commodity, so that some of the $B_{i,j,k}$ may be empty references. The price of $B_{i,j,k}$ for a member j is thus:

$$P_{i,j,k} \equiv \begin{cases} \text{acquisition price for } B_{i,j,k} & \text{if } B_{i,j,k} \text{ exists} \\ 0 & \text{otherwise} \end{cases}$$

where the acquisition price is the price paid in its own currency by a member (including the federal entity) to acquire that particular block. We then define:

$E_j \equiv$ the exchange rate of member currency j
in terms of the federal currency;
[0 is the index of the federal unit, so $E_0 \equiv 1$]

$F_{i,j,k} \equiv$ the price in federal currency of $B_{i,j,k}$ for $i \in [1,n]$, $j \in [0,m]$ and $k \in [1,b]$; and

$M_i \equiv$ the price in federal currency of commodity i for the current session of the market.

Thus we note that:

$$F_{i,j,k} = E_j \cdot P_{i,j,k}$$

and that member j or the federal entity will be willing to sell $B_{i,j,k}$ in that session of the market only if:

$$M_i \geqslant F_{i,j,k}$$

or, equivalently, when:

$$M_i \geqslant E_j \cdot P_{i,j,k}$$

A selection of the blocks of commodity I which member J or the federal entity would be willing and able to sell at the price M_i would then be the set:

$$\text{Sell}(I,J) = \{B_{I,J,k}, k \in [1,b] : P_{I,J,k} \neq 0 \land E_J \cdot P_{I,J,k} \leqslant M_I\}$$

with the actual supply being a subset of that selection:

$$\text{Supply}(I) \subseteq \bigcup_{j=1}^{m} \text{Sell}(I,j)$$

That subset is constrained by the fact that the supply of a commodity for a market session, the quantity of that commodity supplied for its transactions, must be equal to the demand satisfied for it in that same session.

In considering demand, we start by specifying r as the size of the reserve that each member is to hold of each listed commodity. This value, which is less than b, then defines a partition of the storage into those for *reserve* blocks and those for *produce* blocks, as well as another value: the maximum number of *produce* blocks for each participant: p. We then adopt the convention of designating the first r storage areas of a participant as being for the *reserve* blocks, with the remaining areas being designated for the *produce* blocks. For ease of expression, we will refer to these storage areas with the blocks meant to be stored in them. An empty block reference in the $B_{i,j,k}$ then corresponds to a physically empty storage area which is available for an actual block. We then define the reserve of commodity I for member J as the set:

$$\text{Reserve}(I, J) \equiv \{B_{I,J,k}, k \in [1,r] : B_{I,J,k} \text{ is not empty}\}$$

The reserve requirement of commodity I for member J is therefore:

$$\left|\text{Reserve}(I, J)\right| = r$$

This is only a requirement for opting out of demanding a block of a commodity for a given session. In that sense, it is a goal for the market and the reason for its existence. If a session starts for a federal market where all of the reserve requirements are met, including those of the federal entity in the next market up, and there are no distributor orders to take blocks out of reserve, then there is no reason for that session to continue and it can stop immediately. Indeed, if there is a lack of demand for a commodity, from the members, from the federal entity and through the distributors, then the session can be simplified by excluding that commodity from its operation. It is only for those commodities for which members have not met their requirements that a federal market would run a session. However, that is unlikely for any commodity with significant use in an economy. Those members who consume but do not produce that commodity and those members facing a sudden need for it, will eventually need to replenish their stocks of it by drawing on their reserves through their distributors, thereby creating a demand for that commodity and giving need for a market session trading on it. Without significant use, a commodity should be delisted.

There are also commodities, such as grain, for which there is a regular need and, for that reason, will not cease trading for any appreciable length of time. For those, we might worry about the opposite scenario of not having a chance of building up reserves with only one block being purchased in a session. Those worries are quickly allayed by noting that, since each block is sufficient to meet the weekly needs of a member for its commodity, only one session in a week would have to be devoted to replenishing stocks, with the other three or four sessions devoted to building up reserves. There is therefore no hardship in restricting the demand during a single session from a single member for a single commodity to at most one block.[1]

The actual state of affairs would be a balance,

---

[1] Doing so allows greater fluidity of price movements, as it distributes spikes in demand over several sessions and then, as these spikes seek an outlet in other markets, several federal levels. Increases in supply of this *hot* commodity can then come from across the entire federal network of markets, avoiding any overproduction when its demand subsides and assuring a more even distribution of productive capacity if its demand persists.

The Treasuries, Trade, Aid and War

with the reserve creating an assured demand for a given commodity, as long as its requirement has not been fully met, and slowing down the market after that point to gracefully handle the ebb and flow of consumption while being prepared to meet the urgent needs brought on by calamities. The number of blocks of commodity I demanded by members, d_I, would therefore be at most m, the number of members, and kept close to m for many sessions by reserve requirements and internal demand. This demand from the members would then be augmented by the demand, f_I, of the federal entity for blocks of I to sell to the wider market through buying *produce* blocks. As mentioned above, f_I would never be more than seven. If Demand(I) is the demand for I as realized in the blocks of I sold in the current market session for this federal union, then we have:

$$d_I \leqslant m \;,\; f_I \leqslant 7 \text{ and } |\text{Demand}(I)| = d_I + f_I$$

$$\text{so: } |\text{Demand}(I)| \leqslant m+7$$

and, since supply must equal demand, we also have:

$$|\text{Supply}(I)| = d_I + f_I \text{ and } |\text{Supply}(I)| \leqslant m+7$$

Now, if we view the federal market as a trading vehicle, then the supply of a commodity by a member is its physical export of that commodity. By the definition of Supply, above, the supply of commodity I by member J is shown to be:

$$\text{Supply}(I, J) = \text{Sell}(I, J) \cap \text{Supply}(I)$$

To express exports in terms of a member currency, we multiply the the number of blocks of each commodity supplied by the member, by the market price in terms of the member currency. The market price defined above, M_i, is in terms of the federal currency, so we multiply it by the reciprocal of its member-to-federal exchange rate to perform the reverse conversion from federal-to-member currency. Since multiplying by a reciprocal is the same as dividing, the exports of commodity I by member J are therefore:

$$\text{Exports}(I, J) = \frac{M_I}{E_J} \cdot \left| \text{Supply}(I, J) \right|$$

The total exports for member J would then be:

$$\text{Exports}(J) = \sum_{i=1}^{n} \frac{M_i}{E_J} \cdot \left| \text{Supply}(i, J) \right|$$

Similarly, we note that, as long as a member has not met the reserve requirements for a commodity in a market session, it will have a demand in that session for one block of that commodity. Therefore, the demand for commodity I by member J will be:

$$\text{Demand}(I, J) = \begin{cases} \{\text{one } B_{I,x,y}\} & \text{if } |\text{Reserve}(I,J)| < r \\ \emptyset & \text{otherwise} \end{cases}$$

Noting that the member currency spent by any one member on its demand for a given commodity in a market session is its imports of that commodity in terms of its member currency, we have:

$$\text{Imports}(I, J) = \frac{M_I}{E_J} \cdot |\text{Demand}(I, J)|$$

or, noting that $\text{Demand}(I, J)$ is either a singleton or the empty set, we can reduce this to:

$$\text{Imports}(I, J) = \begin{cases} \dfrac{M_I}{E_J} & \text{if } |\text{Reserve}(I,J)| < r \\ 0 & \text{otherwise} \end{cases}$$

The total imports for member J would then be:

$$\text{Imports}(J) = \sum_{i=1}^{n} \frac{M_i}{E_J} \cdot |\text{Demand}(i, J)|$$

for a net currency flow in the federal market of:

$$\text{Net}(J) = \sum_{i=1}^{n} \frac{M_i}{E_J} \cdot \left(\left| \text{Supply}(i,J) \right| - \left| \text{Demand}(i,J) \right| \right)$$

If we let C_J be the inflow (+) or outflow (-) of member currency J from an exogenous currency exchange and $Carryover(J)$ be the carryover of currency flows for member J from the previous session, then the new carryover of currency flows for member J from this session would be:

$$Carryover'(J) = Net(J) + C_J + Carryover(J)$$

It would then be the goal of the market logic to reduce the magnitude of this new carryover for the member with the most imbalanced currency flows. Specifically, by setting suitable market prices, exchange rates and supply subsets, we seek to make minimal the largest carryover:

$$max(\{ \left| Carryover'(j) \right| : j \in [1, m] \})$$

Note that these determinations can be made without the explicit choices of the members involved. As long as the market prices M_i and exchange rates

E_j are set fairly and all trades benefit each member involved in the trade, there should be no objection to these being automated in the federal market. For its participants are federal entities rather than people and its goal is to build up reserves of various commodities for each *polis* rather than to satisfy individual tastes.

But what of the members who are able to sell a commodity below the market price? Should not they be able to sell themselves the one block they are required to buy at that lower price? Why, yes, they should and they can without disturbing the current market price or limiting the supply of that commodity. Everybody who is selling that commodity is still selling it in the same quantities as before and each block beyond the one for self-sale is being sold at the market price. There is no change in net transfer of funds from buying and selling that one block at the market price versus buying and selling at another price. It is netted out in the calculation of the $Net(j)$ for each commodity, where one block is deducted for import from the export blocks, if any. There is no change except the ability of members to preserve the lower prices for their own reserve blocks of commodities, typically produced by those members, themselves. It is only fair that if a block of a commodity is produced by a member and sold to the federal distributor at one price but not actually traded to another member, then the price upon returning to that distributor for local sale should not be increased on account of passing through a market without incident. On the other hand, if those blocks should find their way back to the trading blocks, the buyers of commodities may find that the availability of blocks at their original prices lowers the market prices at that time.

The only concern here, the only issue of fairness, is in not breaking the market by allowing a more expensive block to supplant a cheaper one in export. The unfairness is prevented by having only one set of market prices, M_i, and in allowing all sellers to sell at that price if they can profit from it, thus by only allowing blocks valued above the market price for a commodity to be excluded from the supply of that commodity. For each commodity, then, its market price on a given session must be the least block value for which the number of filled blocks of equal or lesser value is at least the size of the demand. In notation, M_I, the market price for the commodity I would be:

$$min(\{F_{I,j,k} : \left| \left\{ B_{I,j',k'} : \begin{matrix} P_{I,j',k'} \neq 0 \land \\ F_{I,j',k'} \leq F_{I,j,k} \end{matrix} \right\} \right| \geq d_I + f_I \})$$

where $F_{i,j,k} = E_j \cdot P_{i,j,k}$,
d_I = demand for commodity I from the members and
f_I = demand for commodity I from the federal entity.

From this we can see that a market price of M_I only allows for the supply to be a strict subset of the market price selection, $Supply(I) \subset Sel(I)$, when the market price is shared by two or more blocks. However, in that case, the sellers of those blocks neither gain nor lose from the sale, so they are ambivalent about their blocks being included or excluded from the supply. Since these blocks are the most expensive of the selection, none of them can be supplanted by a more expensive one. Consequently, the market cannot be broken for I or any other commodity on the exchange.

Another measure which might be used to select the blocks to export is comparative advantage. In this context of trading blocks of commodities, we start by relating the price of a filled block $B_{I,J,K}$ of member J to the price of some other filled block $B_{i,J,k}$ of that same member in a ratio of the cheapness of the given block $B_{I,J,K}$ compared to that other block:

$$R(J,I,K,i,k) \equiv \begin{cases} \dfrac{P_{I,J,K}}{P_{i,J,k}} & \text{where } P_{I,J,K} \neq 0 \neq P_{i,J,k} \\ 1 & \text{otherwise} \end{cases}$$

The product of the cheapness ratios for $B_{I,J,K}$ relative to all filled blocks of J gives us an aggregate measure of the cheapness of $B_{I,J,K}$ within J's trading universe:

$$\prod_{i=1}^{n} \prod_{k=1}^{b} R(J,I,K,i,k)$$

Note that the product is not changed by the inclusion of the ratio $R(J,I,K,I,K)$. This product can then be normalized into a geometric mean by taking its B_J^{th} root, where B_J is the total number of filled blocks J has available to trade. The resulting value thus denotes the local advantage (LA) of the block $B_{I,J,K}$ in a manner comparable to the contexts of other members:

$$LA(J,I,K) \equiv \sqrt[B_J]{\prod_{i=1}^{n}\prod_{k=1}^{b} R(J,I,K,i,k)}$$

Finally, we construct a geometric mean from the ratios of the local advantage of $B_{I,J,K}$ to the local advantages of all filled blocks of commodity I (numbering T_I) to come up with the comparative advantage (CA) of buying $B_{I,J,K}$ in the context of this market session:

$$CA(J,I,K) \equiv \begin{cases} \sqrt[T_I]{\prod_{\substack{j\in[1,m] \wedge \\ k\in[1,b]}}^{P_{I,J,k}\neq 0} \dfrac{LA(J,I,K)}{LA(j,I,k)}} & \text{where } P_{I,J,K}\neq 0 \\ 1 & \text{otherwise} \end{cases}$$

From Ricardian trade theory, we would expect that the tradable blocks of a commodity with the best comparative advantages (lowest $CA(J,I,K)$) would be the blocks of that commodity traded in an internal balance of trade for this market. As the Ricardian model relies upon the exchange rates and market prices to effect this balance, we look to the equations above to derive the exchange rates of the member currencies relative to the federal currency. The mechanism described earlier then determines the market price, with the selection of the supply from among commodity blocks tied at the market price adjusting trade closer to balance. Toward this end, we first reduce the equations, making them more useful by canceling out any common factors which might otherwise obscure the essential factors in setting the exchange rates.

Starting with the local advantage definition:

$$LA(J,I,K) = \begin{cases} \sqrt[B_J]{\prod_{i \in [1,n] \wedge k \in [1,b]}^{P_{i,J,k} \neq 0} \dfrac{P_{I,J,K}}{P_{i,J,k}}} & \text{where } P_{I,J,K} \neq 0 \\ 1 & \text{otherwise} \end{cases}$$

we note that the number of factors is B_J so that:

$$LA(J,I,K) = \begin{cases} \dfrac{\sqrt[B_J]{P_{I,J,K}^{B_J}}}{\sqrt[B_J]{\prod_{i \in [1,n] \wedge k \in [1,b]}^{P_{i,J,k} \neq 0} P_{i,J,k}}} & \text{where } P_{I,J,K} \neq 0 \\ 1 & \text{otherwise} \end{cases}$$

The numerator reduces to $P_{I,J,K}$. The denominator can be thought of as the member price level (MPL) for J's tradable blocks:

$$MPL(J) \equiv \sqrt[B_J]{\prod_{i \in [1,n] \wedge k \in [1,b]}^{P_{i,J,k} \neq 0} P_{i,J,k}}$$

The local advantage thus reduces to:

$$LA(J,I,K) = \begin{cases} \dfrac{P_{I,J,K}}{MPL(J)} & \text{where } P_{I,J,K} \neq 0 \\ 1 & \text{otherwise} \end{cases}$$

A similar reduction on comparative advantage derives:

$$CA(J,I,K) = \begin{cases} \dfrac{LA(J,I,K)}{\sqrt[T_I]{\prod\limits_{\substack{j \in [1,m] \wedge \\ k \in [1,b]}}^{P_{I,j,k} \neq 0} LA(j,I,k)}} & \text{where } P_{I,J,K} \neq 0 \\ 1 & \text{otherwise} \end{cases}$$

The denominator may be described as the commodity advantage level CAL of the commodity I blocks:

$$CAL(I) \equiv \sqrt[T_I]{\prod_{\substack{j \in [1,m] \wedge \\ k \in [1,b]}}^{P_{I,j,k} \neq 0} LA(j,I,k)}$$

Substituting for the local advantage with the reduction above and for the geometric mean of local advantages for a commodity with its commodity advantage level as just defined, results in the formula:

$$CA(J,I,K) = \begin{cases} \dfrac{P_{I,J,K}}{MPL(J) \cdot CAL(I)} & \text{where } P_{I,J,K} \neq 0 \\ 1 & \text{otherwise} \end{cases}$$

Keeping in mind that the advantage is one of being able

to produce a good more cheaply, this equation tells us that the comparative advantage of an actual block of a commodity held by a member is the ratio of the block's cheapness, compared to the other blocks of its member, over its commodity's level of cheapness overall compared to that of other commodities. A comparative advantage of one is thus of something neither cheap nor dear, and is therefore a fitting value to give to a block which is not there.

Returning to the goal of showing that market pricing achieves selection by comparative advantage, we note that the ordering of the blocks of a commodity by their federal price determined which were sold and which were not, with the sole exception of those blocks priced exactly at the market price. If we were to show that this is the same ordering as that of comparative advantage, then we will have shown that market pricing indeed achieves selection by comparative advantage. Now a sufficient, though not obviously necessary, condition of two orderings being identical is that their values are proportional. The empty blocks need not be considered, but we can assign them the market price after the fact and include them in the gray zone of those blocks for which a sale provides neither gain nor loss. This is analogous to their being neither cheap nor dear with a comparative advantage of one.

Our next step is to show the proportionality of the federal price with the comparative advantage of a block, which we do by positing it in order to compute what its value should be. Letting q_I be the multiplier of this proportion for commodity I, we have:

$$E_J \cdot P_{I,J,K} = \frac{P_{I,J,K} \cdot q_I}{MPL(J) \cdot CAL(I)} \quad where P_{I,J,K} \neq 0$$

$$M_I = q_I \qquad otherwise$$

and eliminating the common factor of the block price in the first equation, we simply it to:

$$E_j = \frac{q_I}{MPL(j) \cdot CAL(I)}.$$

Since there is only one exchange rate E_j for each member j, there must be for that member a common multiplier, s_j, such that:

$$s_j = \frac{q_1}{CAL(1)} = \cdots = \frac{q_n}{CAL(n)}$$

Yet the s_j are, by these equations, invariant across members, so they must all be equal to the common multiplier, s. The exchange rates would then be:

$$E_j = \frac{s}{MPL(j)}$$

This equation, though, immediately suggests what s is, the federal price level (FPL), which can be readily seen from the restatement:

$$E_j \cdot MPL(j) = FPL \text{ for each member } j.$$

In other words, converting the price level of a member into federal currency is the federal price level. Thus, we also derive a formula for the proportion multipliers:

$$q_I = FPL \cdot CAL(I),$$

indicating that the ranking of blocks for a given commodity by prices in terms of federal currency and by comparative advantage are equivalent after adjusting for the federal price and commodity advantage levels. Also, the market price of commodity I is the price of an actual block in terms of the federal currency:

$$M_I = F_{I, j_m, k_m} \text{ where } B_{I, j_m, k_m} \text{ is not empty}$$

and thus:

$$M_I = \frac{FPL \cdot P_{I, j_m, k_m}}{MPL(j_m)}.$$

Since, from the definition of CA, we have:

$$P_{I, j_m, k_m} = CA(j_m, I, k_m) \cdot MPL(j_m) \cdot CAL(I),$$

we can substitute and reduce to get:

$$M_I = FPL \cdot CA(j_m, I, k_m) \cdot CAL(I).$$

Finally, we observe that a block priced at the market price for its commodity has a comparative advantage, or cheapness ratio, of one. We can therefore reduce this to:

$$M_I = FPL \cdot CAL(I) \quad \text{and} \quad M_I = q_I,$$

the latter being the equation of proportionality for the empty blocks. We conclude that comparative advantage and market prices are proportional by a factor of q_I and therefore establish the same ordering of blocks.

Note that these equations are true regardless of the formal exchange rates. We have calculated their relationship with other factors but have not set them in the exposition of comparative advantage and market pricing. The engine of equilibrium in each federal economy, inclusive of entrepreneurial markets, and its mechanism for keeping formal exchange rates within hailing distance of their real counterparts, is found in picking the minimum largest carryover over a set of alternatives. One might be tempted to come up with a general solution until confronted with the complexity of the intra-market calculations and the unpredictability of the extra-market components of the carryovers. A more sensible path is to limit the change in the exchange rates to a small, fixed amount up or down, or no change at all. Even with these limited options, the computation becomes unwieldy for larger memberships, as do other matters; the Iroquois had it about right at five or six members. Setting the amount of the adjustment at a cent of the federal currency unit allows a maximum movement of two-and-a-half federal currency units up or down in a year with 250 trading sessions. This seems a reasonable limit to the annual fluctuation in an exchange rate, but a federal market may have reasons for a different tick size. Whatever is chosen for membership and tick size, the mechanism is the same: Take the 3^m adjustments, remove the impossible or prohibited ones, and compute:

$$max(\{|\text{Carryover}'(j)|: j \in [1, m]\})$$

for each and pick the adjustment with the least such largest carryover.

As a practical matter, in a world with whole countries enslaved by debt to the extent of their governments being told not to serve their citizens lest they fail to make a loan payment, the debt as carryover is reduced for the extreme cases until it is cleared for all governments. This transition begins with debt between the trading partners being prohibited, so that future debt will not corrupt trade going forward. The existing debt will create a flow of funds from borrower to lender that will be imports by borrowers and exports by lenders of debt retirement. The federal market will balance this flow with another of exports by borrowers and imports by lenders of real commodities. From the perspective of mercantilism which so pervades the dominant news, it would appear that those who were once exporter nations are now firmly importer nations, while those who were forever importer nations are now resurgent exporter nations. Certainly, the ill-gotten productive capacity of the formerly exporter countries will sit idle or will be redirected to other uses, while countries once without any industry of their own will seem to bloom with factories. What is really happening, though, is that the countries are finding their productive centers and are benefiting each other by engaging themselves where they have a comparative advantage. They are being helped in that direction by undoing the damage done by decades of mercantilism and debt, in fact propelled by the unwinding of the entanglements of loans.

This can be accomplished, moreover, without eliminating the currency which is blamed for the crisis in Europe. As the previous discussion makes clear, it is not the presence of euros, but the absence of drachma and marks which is to blame. An implementation of a federal market in Europe will require a euro as a trading currency, as much as it needs the retention of member currencies. In fact, it will require several euros so that the European Union can be recast in a more manageable federal form, with regional sub-unions with no more than six members in each of those. This reformulation of the EU may result in Greece paying back its debt through a sub-union while Germany is its own sub-union. Whole regions can be revitalized when one of its countries pays back its debt, the imbalance in drachma being rendered as an imbalance of a Balkan currency with the mark. Eventually, though, this all settles down into a world without debt, the people in the villages and the institutions in each instance of the *polis* at every level finding a comfortable balance and rhythm of life.

Now that we have discussed, at some length, how the treasuries and trade within a federalist state can enable comity, both in the ideal and the particular case, we will turn briefly to the matter of foreign aid. For there seems little reason to dwell on something which serves little if any purpose once commodity reserves and exchanges are in place. Rarely is the devastation wrought by a disaster so complete that the network of reserves made available by trade would prove inadequate to the task. Even the loss of skilled civil servants, such as doctors and engineers, can be handled by immigration of those professionals into the afflicted region, working in positions paid at the highest federal level.

It should be noted, as well, that the disaster is usually the result of decisions made within the afflicted region and, though the victims themselves might not have been the instigators of those decisions, the parties receiving and distributing the aid almost always are. We are thus presented, whenever aid is offered by governments trying to relieve the distress of the people from natural and man-made disasters, with a disgusting spectacle of graft, violence and waste in its distribution. Religious groups fare better in this regard, especially when they can count as members some of the disaster victims and when they are already connected through the administration of their faith. Best of all, though, are those approaches which help the people structure their civic organization so that they can help themselves.

This is precisely what has been offered in this book or what is hoped has been offered. The formation into self-sufficient colleges of extended families, each with their own farm on which they grow their own food, combined then into wards and villages, then into cities and higher federal levels, is a process which starts at a local level where there is still some local control and is therefore most accessible to the poor in the forgotten backwaters of the world. Here the people are themselves least accessible to organized aid, as well as being, arguably, most in need of aid. It may seem trite, but it is shown by such considerations to be true, that the greatest aid is an idea.

Response to Possible Objections

Response to Possible Objections

The superficial resemblance of the provision to a welfare program is likely to open Popular Capitalism to charges or claims of being socialist. That bureaucracy, *welfare of the middle class*, or government posts, *welfare of the campaign worker*, or labor unions, *welfare of the untrainable*, fail to conjure up such notions is perhaps due to the instant-thinking of our time, where impressions speak louder than the truth. Nonetheless, this misconception gives me the opportunity to show just how opposite Popular Capitalism is to Socialism in its effect. Its opposition in philosophy is seen from my rejection, at the very outset, of the myth of a public person possessing a general will[1], from which notion of Rousseau modern Socialism

---

1 [ROUSSEAU] pp.28-29, where Rousseau maintains that the sovereignty of the people is indivisible, asserting toward that end a general and hence indivisible will of the people.

and a host of more destructive ideologies, Communism and Fascism among them, have their root.[1]

Socialism is the remote governmental control of the economy and people's lives in the hope that, under this management, life for the poor and most others will improve. What I am proposing would entail less control of the people. Economic control would mostly be removed, as provision replaces regulation. Control over people would be lessened by removing the entitlements, which places the poor at the mercy of claims examiners, and by ending the tax of survival costs, which depletes daily the economic power of individuals.

---

[1] Rousseau [ROUSSEAU] equates the general will of the people with the will of the majority when he writes, in a footnote, "that a will may be general, it is not always necessary that it should be unanimous, but it is necessary that all votes should be counted", thus excluding the will of the people in the minority at any level of association or scope. Rousseau was so worried about dividing sovereignty that he absurdly combined scope into a stifling dictatorship of the majority at the highest levels. To his metaphor, of the sovereign body cut apart and then monstrously re-assembled, can be replied another, of a body having no involuntary functions and no separation into systems, so that the lung cannot breathe, the stomach cannot digest and the muscles of a limb cannot expand and contract in a coordinated manner without a conscious decision in the brain. For a more concrete rendering of how the will of the majority leads to tyranny by a few and slavery for the rest, see [HAYEK].

Response to Possible Objections

To be sure, a possibly remote government will, in the second form of the provision, be more involved in certain industries than before, even as it ends its interference in other industries. As a supplier, it charges no price, gains no profit and reaps no benefit from its supplying. Rather, it is giving power away, enhancing the power of others to live free. We see nothing sinister in the fire department and other cases of a government supplying a service. Why should we be worried here? As a buyer, it is only one, albeit large, buyer among others. Once its economy, encouraged by the provision, expands beyond survival, the influence of a government as buyer will lessen. Popular Capitalism results in less remote control of the people in this case, as well.

Other industries must be operating in order to fulfill the provision, in order to supply the commodities needed to operate it. Our public representatives may later assert that this can only be assured if a widely scoped and thus remote government was the sole manufacturer of those goods. This would be suspect reasoning. The great demand of government at every level practically assures that the industries they need will not go under and urban federalism assures that investment by the colleges in each village can easily begin or resume those industries locally. Even if that were a realistic danger at present and we allowed for government manufacturing of goods in an essentially private market, these governments would be merely persistent competitors, ones which will stay in business when others fail and thus resist the efforts for private monopoly. There is no need for any government to establish monopolies for itself simply to assure supplies of a good. Companies can be owned by the members of a federal union and thus avoid the danger of monopoly.

Moreover, federated sovereignty in land implies ownership of its resources by either the members of a federal union on the land within their sovereignty or by the federal union's government over land under their federal jurisdiction. To abdicate that control is a breach of the federal agreement to cede control over some land and resources for the mutual benefit of all members of the federal union. Resources in the domain of a federal union must be exploited by just that federal union, with civil servants extracting the resource and civil servants selling the resource to its members and companies, with all proceeds being federal union revenue. To pawn off any or all of this activity onto private entities, whether foreign or domestic, suggests that the resources are not in a domain, but owned by cronies of those in power. Popular Capitalism is not socialism in this regard, but simply not cronyism and not fraud.

Another example of disinvolvement by federal governments concerns the funding of the provision, where the manipulation of private investment through the regulation of private banks is replaced by a federal system of judicial banks which are forbidden to invest, as well as the greater protection offered to their depositors' well-being offered by the provision. Prohibitions against long-term loans and service fee insurance, indeed of any financial contract which serves to inflate prices while subjugating the people, are then directly enforced by the internal regulation of these judicial banks so that the provision may then have its full effect in freeing the people from poverty and obligation. Then, as the provision makes wage income unnecessary in achieving that same liberation, any intrusion into private decisions to consume or to invest also becomes unnecessary.

Thus, the expansion of Congressional powers under the Commerce Clause will also be indefensible as the argument in Wickard v. Filburn, which allowed that expansion, will become patently absurd rather than merely suspect. Indeed, under the urban federalism of Popular Capitalism, the interstate economy consists solely of trade between the states and an exchange of their currencies, *interstate commerce* in its proper sense. To mandate or forbid the purchases or possessions of any individual, family, college, ward, local institution, village or city will not affect this true interstate commerce because no state would be involved in those purchases or would be affected in its commerce by any of these parties possessing any given good. The federal market at the present federal level would be the only form of regulation for interstate commerce and, as with all trading systems, its regulation would be beneficial for all of its participants, in this case the states. That would be a rarity in the external regulation of other entities by government.

Response to Possible Objections

Moreover, requiring states to purchase any one particular product outside of comparative advantage or their decisions to list or not list commodities, while affecting interstate commerce, will not promote general welfare but, instead, hinder it, as David Ricardo well demonstrated. Free trade between the states is required for comparative advantage to bring the mutual benefits of that trade to each state. Forced purchase will destroy those advantages at every level where it is employed. Therefore, forced purchases under our current scheme, where the state economies are not separated but chained together by a common currency, eliminates any benefits to the general welfare which might have been received from foreign trade. This is one reason why some states are wealthy and others languish in abject poverty.

If that was not enough to discredit the regulation of the people, the specific ways in which the general welfare was claimed to have benefited from intrusion into consumer decisions are already handled by Popular Capitalism without such assaults on personal liberty. The curtailing of the wheat market under the New Deal was done to maintain the income of the farmers so that they would be able to survive and produce food; under Popular Capitalism, the demand for food is monetized through the provision and grown by the colleges for their members' own nourishment and benefit first, with only the excess entering trade. Requiring individuals to buy health insurance under *Obamacare* was intended to assure access to medical care to everyone; under Popular Capitalism, medical care is directly provided to everyone who needs it by the colleges and the *polis* at each level, eventually, and by Municipal Medical Departments, in the meantime, in either case without the health insurance middleman.

With less government involvement comes less government expenses, so that the provision is easier to finance. However, the most substantial budgetary cuts, besides the programs that the provision replaces, are in an area where total government dis-involvement is not politically feasible: defense. I do not accept it, however, as an essential duty of government. The present authority of government need not be slackened by an impending invasion. No invader will find cooperation from the invaded if a government still holds some

Response to Possible Objections

esteem. The invader, in any event, needs to establish his own authority. As for the safety of citizens, if the danger is outside the control of this government, might it not lie outside all possible governmental control? Why is it necessary, then, to expect the impossible?

This last point shows where we may contain some costs. Frequently, the military is used to protect citizens or property overseas, these being somewhat grandiloquently called national interests. However, only a few people and industries are affected, and these gladly took the risk of setting up shop or home in a foreign land, outside the sovereignty of their native government. Why, then, should those who have shown the better part of valor by staying home, where their government is better equipped to protect them, be forced to pay for those who take outlandish risks? Economic sense alone says that those who risk must pay the price as well as reap the reward. The costs of protecting foreign operations and travelers should thus be borne by those businesses and tourists and not by their native government. That government then has a choice of abandoning their protection or continuing it under contract, with the protected persons paying a fee that is profitable for the government and the people. Either way, the net military expenses of government are significantly reduced.

We should also be wary of paranoid views of national security. If a government sought to protect itself from every conceivable way to overthrow it, every imaginable threat, there would be no end to military expense. Perhaps, if we took a better look at our enemies' weaknesses and the difficulties they would face in trying to hurt us, we would come up with a more realistic estimate of the actual threat they pose. Such an investigation would also improve our strategy against them to render them incapable of attacking us, if that is what we have been led to fear.

Further, those who insist on dire prophecies are less inclined to accept the efforts of allies. There is more danger, after all, if they are not quite on our side. Of course, this distrust brings the fulfillment of that prophecy. Who can be fond of an arrogant ally, one who takes no advice from us, trying to do everything itself? The less authority and responsibility we give our allies, the more we turn the allied concerns into our concerns, our worries and our duty. Conversely, if we entrust more authority and responsibility to our allies, letting them participate in our mutual defense, we can more easily convince them to bear a greater share of its cost.

Even when these reductions of costs, the growth in the economy and the prospect of establishing an endowment are considered, some might be concerned that expectations of currency-printing which is to create the endowment and initially finance the provision will bring inflation. This would be no problem, if it were so, but a blessing. Inflation devalues our sizable debts. Since the policy would not take on new debts, instead paying the whole of expenditures and some portion of the old debt, the total debt can not increase. Moreover, the increased prices will just mean that we pay farmers more, as well as food service workers. Both could use the money. And when the farmers earn more, they can repay their loans instead of defaulting. The banks are happy; the farmers and food service workers are happy; other creditors are taxed, but this is offset by fewer defaults; those on fixed incomes have another, better way of living day to day; those with real assets see their value increase; those who have currency lose out, but they also can make use of the provision, so it is not a total loss for them either. There are no irrecoverable disasters and most people are happier. Finding another public of such general benefit would be difficult.

The only worry might be that hyper-inflation will wreck the economy before the policy can take effect. This also is much ado about nothing. First of all, hyper-inflation is not likely. By steadfastly reducing its debt, government assures that there will be less to repay in the future. As the government builds its endowment, the percentage of expenditures paid by the income from the endowment will increase and there will be less need of new currency for further building. Full endowment, taking inflation into consideration, would end the need for more currency; over-endowment would mean that government could remove currency from the system. The prospect of these anti-inflationary measures, which the market would have to discount, dampens inflation before it occurs. Therefore, while the overall growth in prices may be large, steady movement toward a deflationary position would discourage the inflationary expectations which create hyper-inflation. Compare this with our present policy of keeping inflation low but building debts and thus inflationary expectations to absurd heights. Which is most likely to throw us into hyper-inflation?

My second comment on this score is that hyper-inflation is not a great menace for Popular Capitalism. Industry might be thrashing about, but people will not starve. Indeed, industry will be propped up, when depression hits, by the steady demand for commodities needed to effect the provision and the buying power of those who the government pays, directly or indirectly, to provide it. The provision builds up economic power at all times, of course, so it is fighting depression constantly, even before it occurs. Thus, depression after hyper-inflation is less likely under Popular Capitalism. But if it does come, the means of relief are already in place and working. Popular Capitalism could probably have taken the Great Depression in stride.

Of course, there are those who see Inflation as their dragon, the only monster they need to destroy.

They make its slaying the sole goal of their policy. They do not realize that its absence is a bookkeeping nicety at best, and that its presence is a red herring, distracting us from the real culprit: fixed income schemes. Others judge all things by productivity, which treasure they would gain at whatever peril. With national income accounts in hand, they preach their message of GNP-ism: that the over-productive will inherit the earth, that evolution favors those who make more things or similar nonsense in the rhetoric in current use. If triumphant, they use their Bragonomics to proclaim:

> *My way's better than your way*
> *My way's better than yours*
> *My way's better than your way*
> *It says so here in the figures*

There are of course several other measures one might use to gauge the performance of the economy. Most real economists use a large sample of these. However, even these are biased towards a view that more is better, or are tied up in the structural assumptions of the present system. Unemployment, for example, is seen as a scourge because the survival of most people is currently dependent on their continual employment. If unemployment were more a choice in wealth than an affliction towards poverty, we would welcome rather than dread its increase. We would call it vacation and add it to our *pleasure measure*. Reporters would wait outside the Department of Fun for the latest Vacation Report and give distressing accounts if it fell below twenty percent.

Seriously, though, to dismiss Popular Capitalism because it does not satisfy the zealots of one measure or another is unreasonable. No policy but maximizing one measure would gain the approval of its adherents, while it loses the approval of the fanatics of other measures. Rather, policies should be analyzed with both many measures and the good sense to see what they mean in different circumstances. The result of this analysis will not be a pithy, one-line sound bite that misleads as it entertains the unaware. It will, in fact, bore most people to tears before they switch their attention to the next episode of *Really Vacuous People*. For those who really want to understand our economic reality, though, it will be far more enlightening than any single measure.

Now I am no enemy of measures *per se*. I do object, though, to them being used as a substitute for reasoning. My methodology, in this regard, follows that of Henry George[1], in treating political economics as a theoretical science, where logical analysis rules over the empirical. The criticisms which baldly state that none of my proposals will *work*, based on some study or an

---

1 In a Veblenesque passage, George provides a keen insight into the source of this blind empiricism, as well as the necessity and the ability of the people to discern the logic of economics:

"It is especially true to-day that all large political questions are at bottom economic questions. There is thus introduced into the study of political economy the same disturbing element that setting men by the ears over the study of theology... at one time, at least, so affected even the study of astronomy as to prevent the authoritative recognition of the earth's movement around the sun long after its demonstration. The organization of the political parties, the pride of place and power that they arouse and the strong prejudices they kindle, are always inimical to the search for truth and to the acceptance of truth. [...] Whoever accepts from [the colleges and universities and accredited organs of education and opinion] a chair of political economy must do so under the implied stipulation that he shall not really find what it is his professional business to look for. [...] Yet, if political economy be the one science that cannot be safely left to specialists, the one science of which it is needful for all to know something, it is also the science the ordinary man may most easily study. It requires no tools, no apparatus, no special learning. The phenomena which it investigates need not be sought for in laboratories or libraries; they lie about us, and are constantly thrust upon us. [...] And its processes, which consist mainly in analysis, require only care in distinguishing what is essential from what is merely accidental." [GEORGE ScPolEcon], pp. xxxiv-xxxv

experiment where they were allegedly *tried*, stem from a failure to put empiricism in its proper place under logic. When I investigate these studies and experiments, they never actually try that which they claim to try and never prove what they claim to have proven. Logical flaws in the premises of the experiments assure that the results are meaningless, however accurate the data.

An example of this are some field-studies[1] which claimed to show that the negative income tax as proposed by Milton Friedman[2] would not work. It turns out that what *work* meant to the authors of those studies was to preserve or enhance the incentive to seek employment and to prevent the breakup of the nuclear family, neither of which were objectives of Friedman, though he did argue for them as consequences of a full implementation of the NIT. What the studies actually showed was that replacing one entitlement group (those who meet welfare requirements) with another (those in the sample group) does not achieve the results that one expects from replacing all entitlements with a subsidy like that in the negative income tax. In other words,

---

1 See [ALLEN].
2 See [FRIEDMAN].

these studies told us nothing except to confirm a result already arrived at by reason: only a full implementation will be a *negative income tax*. The reasoning is similar to that used to explain the effect welfare entitlements have on employment: if the wage one is offered for work on a job is not greater than the total cost of working on that job, one does not have an incentive to seek that employment. The cost for the welfare recipient includes the loss of benefits, while the cost for those in the sample group includes the loss of their freedom to do what they wish with their time. Since the group was not universal, even in being limited to a closed economy in a small village, employers could find workers who were not in the sample group, hence under duress, who were willing to work at lower wages than the free workers of the sample group. Which is to say, wages are the work incentives of a free market, so it was the failure of the studies to fully implement a negative income tax over its study area which caused even a lower work incentive for the sample group, rather than any unspecified shortcoming in the negative income tax itself. Even if the studies were to discover a new flaw, we are unlikely to learn of any logical description of it or any proposed remedy. The intent of such studies are, in the main, to discredit any proposal with logically proven benefits for the people, in order for the owners of a political party to maintain their political or economic advantages.

Still, an evil and adulterous generation seeks a measure, so I will suggest a new one: the percentage of people who are independently wealthy. Yes, it reflects a bias in policy, in this case towards the empowering of individuals. Its attractiveness, to Popular Capitalism, would rest on it having a goal where all might benefit, rather than just creditors, corporations, labor unions or some other group of overlords. Keeping track of it, as with other measures, would add to our knowledge of economic performance. However, no single measure can decide the merit of the sundry ways in which an economy can perform. That question is in the province of philosophy. To answer it, we must step back from the wondrous workings of our economic machine and find in the wider world the reason why it runs.

Such concerns, though they have an answer in Truth, are too controversial for human agreement. You will have opinions which you will not relinquish, your faith, as I have mine. If they do not share any common ground, we may have an argument, but not useful discussion. There is a limit, therefore, to how well I may respond to objections. Such will have to stand; I did not persuade. This may be all well and good, for I might have persuaded you to something false. To force all to believe what you say is not a worthy goal. Nor is it worthy to ignore Truth, to not seek it out. Rather, I wish to help us, as best I can, to discover Truth, if only in a search for a better way to govern a flawed people.

Call to Inaction

Call to Inaction

It has been customary for political philosophers to whip up support for their ideas by rousing pep talks. Often this leads to calls to kill, maim and destroy to further the cause, much as coaches carelessly instruct their athletes to do for *alma mater*. In athletics, this hyperbole is treated as an impassioned plea to play harder than you think you can. In politics, it has a distressing tendency to encourage people to actually go out and kill, maim and destroy.

This is not to say that the calls are always put in those words. They can lay submerged in a sea of high-minded prose. All it takes, though, is one mention of moral superiority, one dismissal of opponents as less than human, one judgment that the cause is more important than any one person. For then, the morally inferior are candidates for elimination, opponents for slaughter and innocent bystanders for sacrifice.

This book will have failed of its aim if it has any such effect. I thus take great pains to exclude several actions from the equipment of those who would try to establish the policies endorsed above. In particular, revolt and cruelty I would avoid. These are the tools of hate. I would give and love.

Any form of killing, however rationalized or couched in euphemism, will diminish the value of this policy. Whoever is killed will not have gained from adopting this suggestion, though it is arguable whether they have lost anything compared to other proposals. If it is a net loss, I can only regard it as a loss more costly than any benefit which others gain.

Nonetheless, those who govern are often faced with hard decisions in which somebody always dies or is hurt. There is nothing on earth which justifies such decisions. Even in victory, David wept for Absalom. There are other reasons by which to choose among sorrows. These may be found in religion.

This policy is not a religion and does not purport to replace one. It is a flawed product of a human writer, intended for discussion, revision, testing and correction. Its aim to help must defer to Truth, lest it be not truly help. Direct service to Truth, a Call from God, must therefore take precedence over this cause. Regular communion with Truth, that is prayer for direction, is essential for us all, individually. This necessity is by no means diminished or supplanted by any actions taken on behalf of this program or in the study of it, as it is not diminished or supplanted by any other program or by any religion, their actions or study. Hopefully, this policy informs and leads, by that informing, to a greater ability of each to follow their Call, individually and without exception. That would be a blessing and it is the spirit in which this gift is given.

Bibliography

[MORE] More, Thomas, ed. Edward Surtz, *Utopia*, (Yale University Press, New Haven, 1977). The original is not the perfect world which the name has come to imply, but more a sly critique of English law.

[PLATO] Plato, transl. Benjamin Jowett, ed. Irwin Edman, *The Works of Plato*, (Random House, New York, 1928). The Republic presents an alternative view of the oikos where it is merged with the polis in a bizarre form which has become a nightmare view of socialism.

[ARISTOTLE] Aristotle, transl. T. A. Sinclair, *The Politics*, (Penguin Books, Bungay, 1979). A theory of the polis and the oikos.

[BELLAMY] Bellamy, Edward, *Looking Backward 2000-1887*, (Random House, Inc., New York, 1917). One form of the provision is described in this novel.

[HICKS.J.D.] Hicks, John D, *The Populist Revolt: A History of the Farmer's Alliance*, (University of Nebraska Press, , 1961). Chronicles the Populist movement, including the calls to end the alien owner ship of land and to establish a monetary system based on grain reserves.

[HICKS.J.R.] Hicks, J. R., *Value and Capital: An Inquiry into Some Fundamental Principles of Economic Theory*, (Oxford University Press, Oxford, 1974). The book with the formulae and graphs of Keynesian economics has a discussion of money as a commodity.

[WOODWARD] Woodward, C. Vann, *Tom Watson: Agrarian Rebel*, (Oxford University Press, New York, 1963). A balanced account of the controversial Populist leader that makes very clear the Populist support of greenbacks and the fateful expediency of the Fusion Ticket with the Silverite Bryan.

[DAVIS] Davis, John P., ed. Abram Chayes, *Corporations: A Study of the Origin and Development of Great Business Combinations and of ther Relation tothe Authority of the State*, (Capricorn Books, New York, 1961). An intriguing history of the corporation and its predecessors, including religious communities, municipalities and residential colleges at the universities, with much in common with the colleges in "Popular Capitalism".

[KEFAUVER] Kefauver, Estes, *In a Few Hands: Monopoly Power in America*, (Penguin Books Inc., Baltimore, 1965). Kefauver shows how monopoly power drives up the prices in their industries.

[GEORGE Progess&Poverty] George, Henry, *Progress and Poverty: An Inquiry into the Cause of Industrial Depressions and of Increase of Want with Increase of Wealth, The Remedy*, (Robert Schalkenbach Foundation, New York, 1949). A formative book for me, with a wealth of observations about land when treated as property

[SMITH] Smith, Adam, ed. Edwin Cannan, *An Inquiry into the Nature and Causes of the Wealth of Nations*, (Random House, Inc., New York, 1937). Self-love and business profiting at the expense of the public.

[RICARDO] Ricardo, David, *The Principles of Political Economy and Taxation*, (J. M. Dent & Sons Ltd., London, 1943). A theory of trade using comparative advantage.

[MILL] Mill, John Stuart, ed. Donald Winch, *Principles of Political Economy, with Some of their Applications to Social Philosophy*, (Penguin Books, Ltd., Aylesbury, Bucks, 1970). A formative book for me, with analysis by holding other things equal, caeteris paribus, and the necessity of freedom in the political economy, leaving the longest impression.

[GEORGE FreeTrade] George, Henry, *Protection or Free Trade: An Examination of the Tariff Question, With Especial Regard to the Interests of Labor*, (Robert Schalkenbach Foundation, New York, 1949). Debunks the many myths about trade which yet persist into the present day.

[KEYNES GenTh] Keynes, John Maynard, *The General Theory of Employment, Interest and Money*, (Harcourt, Brace & World, Inc., New York/Chicago/Burlingame, 1964). Keynes' expansive and subtle work which deals with several issues mooted by Popular Capitalism, nonetheless points out how fixed exchange rates provides a practical rationale for mercantilism.

[KEYNES EconConseq] Keynes, John Maynard, *The Economic Consequences of the Peace*, (Harcourt, Brace and Howe, New York, 1920). Keynes' blistering attack on the reparations, showing them to be statistically impossible for Germany to fulfill, includes a call to end inter-ally debt and to establish a free trade union.

[BIBLE] Division of Christian Education of the National Council of the Churches of Christ in the United States of America, *The Holy Bible, Revised Standard Version*, (Thomas Nelson & Sons, New York, 1952 (Old Testament Section)). The grain reserves of Joseph.

[ROUSSEAU] Rousseau, Jean-Jacques, tr. Henry J. Tozer, ed. Lester G. Crocker, *The Social Contract and Discourse on the Origin and Foundation of Inequality Among Mankind*, (Washington Square Press, New York, 1974). The general will of the people is presented.

[HAYEK] Hayek, Frederich A., *The Road to Serfdom*, (The University of Chicago Press, Chicago, 1956). Hayek describes the loss of freedom from "the will of the majority", but only sees individualism as an alternative.

[GEORGE ScPolEcon] George, Henry, ed. Henry George, Jr., *The Science of Political Economy*, (Robert Schalkenbach Foundation, New York, 1962). Economics as a theoretical science.

[FRIEDMAN] Friedman, Milton, ed. Rose D. Friedman, *Capitalism and Friedman*, (The University of Chicago Press, Chicago, 1970). The Negative Income Tax, with its weekly subsidy to all, administered through the payroll tax system, is an ingenious form of the provision, as it could be put into effect immediately.

[ALLEN] Allen, Jodie T., "Negative Income Tax", *The Fortune Encyclopedia of Economics*, ed. David R. Henderson, (Warner Books, New York, 1993). A summation of the results of some misconceived field-tests of the NIT

Topical Index

Advantage
  comparative 339, 351, 353, 355, 356, 359, 362, 375, is to produce goods more cheaply 355, level, commodity 355, local 352-355
Capital
  accounting 199, 200, alienation 193, 194, 200, as cost 194, as derived notion 107, contributions 196, 197, 217, daily life 102, definition 188, financial 193, human 189, idea 189, 237, incremental purchase 218, investment 190, investments 84, local 215, major role 102, municipalities 214, physical 207, profit maximization 203, regular investment 190, 204, resource 190, responsibilities 191, stock market 99, 100, working 190
Capital Contributions
  property 198
Capital Depreciation
  regular investment 200, 201
Capital Investment
  intended risk 97, 98
Capitalism
  crony 42, 44, 110, definition 188, free market 43, 44, industry 243, popular 42, 43, speculation 98, 99, worker 42, 44
City
  enterprises owned by villages 262, individual 263
College
  allegiance 131, architecture 257, as alma mater 131, as legal entity 122, as oikos 114, 119, 120, 124, 141, as shareholder 130, as the people 187, banking 172, blocks 170, branded goods 327, 331, broadcasting 217, capital 188, 191, 194, children of members 152, citizenship 152, companies 204, company 147, compared to company 225, cooking 137, deliveries 170, dining 136, 137, domain 143, 146, 148, 167, 280, ecology 136, education 177, 210, 242, 243, Electoral 273, employment not required 129, federal 245, 252, 256, federal aspect 258, 275, first federal level of land possession 265, formation 257, 364, grows food provision buys 376, guest rooms 140, hallways 55, harmony with polis 143, identity 130, 181, 223, immigrants 153, incentive to admit 154, individual 263, investment 193, 212, 217, 222, 223, 243, investment as model 215, investment decision 184, investment key to recovery 372, legislative and senatorial roles 272, local crops 312, medical care 376, member participation 224, members 123, 124, 134, mixture of crops 312, most accessible to poor 365, niceties 255, Nominator 273, of Abstract Thought 176, of Athletics 176, 177, of Biological Sciences 174, 175, of Social Sciences 173, 174, of the Arts 176, opportunities 184, 241, personal freedom 123, 126-131, 209, property 148, 214, property rights 194, public 172, 184, quorum 153, regular investment 131, rent 132, residential inertia 121, 122, 125, resources 169, revenue 134, rights 287, rotten 123, 153, 154, self-sufficiency 127, services 140, share of provision 137, sharing resources 169, shops 171, socialization 242, supersedes nuclear family 134,

sustainability 254, wages for chores 128, wall 288, walls 143, 154, work 135, 141, 235, zoning 167
College Attendance
no greater income if parents went 89, wage slavery 79
Comparative Advantage
buying vs. making 268, failure 270, identity 294, mutual advantage of trade 319, mutual benefits of trade 375, of one neither cheap nor dear 356, 357, 359, proportional to federal market prices 357-359, requirements 206, selection by 356, vs. factor mobility 329, vs. forced purchase 375
Currency
exchanges 328
Debt
college education 34, directed inflation 34, 89, inflation 88, mortgage 33, 34, national 71, phasing out sovereign 329, speculation 98, student loans 88
Exchange
federal distributor 336
Family
bonds destroyed by law 288, legislator 272, threat from marriage legalization 288
Family Apartment
business 134, rent 138
Federal
concern ends at member walls 258
Federal Entities
financially dependent on members 258, members as individuals 263
Federalism
as inter-independence 256
Immigrant
citizenship 152
Knowledge
certification 177, 178, 278, role of colleges 178
Land

a birthright 280, as domain 191
Municipal Medical Departments
as part of the provision 62, vs. health insurance 376
Physical Capital
leasing 190, markets 205, 212, profits 99
Polis
construction 244
Political Economy
as power system 10, as rule of law 11, as theoretical science 384, avoidance 18, banking 299, confidence 11, corporate abuse 291, cost of maintaining 15, cost of sovereignty 14, 16, 17, demographics 18, 19, federal 207, form 5, viii, governance and laws 16, greater world 315, income growth 31, intimate families 134, of family farm and artisan home 23, of market and consumers 23, operating cost 28, operational cost 21, 22, oxymoron 107, polis and oikos 107, popular 262, power transfers 15, product 49, provision of necessities 51, requirements 22, 23, 27, 28, sovereignty 16, tasks 12, validity of powers in 13, virtue 19, 20
Popular
definition 187
Popular Capital
collective nature 212, definition 191, endowment 194, funding provision 63, maintenance 244, ownership 188, oxymoron 107, populism 110, profit 194, property 115, 148, stewardship 115
Popular Capitalism
as political economy 42, capitalist 97, citizenship 103, companies 101, corporations 290, creation of ideas 240, 241, creators of ideas 237,

dissemination of ideas 238-240, funding provision 63, harmony of polis and oikos 110, implementation 295, implementation of ideas 241, inflation 380, 381, measures 383, 387, medical care 376, of Physical Sciences 175, oikos 151, personal liberty 375, 376, personal wealth 86, 212, 213, poverty 213, productivity 194, property 198, 214, provision of necessities 44, Sub-Treasury Plan 312, tort 29, true capitalism 184, urban federalism 374, villages 290, vs. remote control of people 371, vs. socialism 369, 373, wages 231

Privacy
of college 192

Provision of the Necessities
apartment rent payment to college 138, benefits 51, 52, 61, 95, 96, college shop 132, 138, cost 49, 50, 52, 71, debt 87, 91, debt repayment 101, direct 53, 60, 62, 63, effects 60, 61, 68, ends poverty 130, equality in college 123, 128, feasibility 50, 51, food 59, 60, full 65, funding 63, housing 58, 59, immigration 64, incentives 52, monetary effects 102, operation 48, partial 51, personal freedom 43, personal liberty 128, 129, 134, questions 44, replaces welfare state 42, requirements 47, 50, 51, 53, 63, retirement 86, revenue 95, shelter 54, to pay debts 65, transition 64, 66-68, treasury 96, wage 68, wages 61, 62, weekly payment 64, 65, weekly payments 65, 66

Service Insurance
car repair 34, medical care 33, 34

Sovereignty
alien ownership permitted by debt 145, cost 9, 12, 13, 15-17, 19-21, 29, 259, currency 324, current practice of competing for exploitation of 148, destroyed by debt 322, divisibility 369, federal 262, 279, functions 15, gives right to issue money 172, gives right to own industry 264, home 287, industry 264, 265, land 146, 279, must be bought 9, no inherent right 9, of political economy 16, over currency 322, over industry 263, over land required for stock ownership 146, power transfers 15, powers 13, preservation of, in federalism 262, products 12, protection for 269, protection of, required for trade 263, resources 372, risk outside of 377, vested in political economy 13, walls 269

Transition
housing 155

Travelers
fortnight stays 156

Urban Federalism
starts building from village to city 256

Village
abstract thought 176, alienation 215, arts 176, attacked by motorists 271, bank 172, 310, banks and exchanges 289, bicameral legislature 275, bureaucracy 183, business 183, canal 171, civil servants 178, civility 263, claim to revenues from local business 214, college 262, 272, communications 290, corporation 290, 292, currency 171, 260, 268, 278, 311, currency cycle 254, 268, currency independence 260, currency placeholder for college provision 260, domain 193, 194, 292, domain accretion 265, education 177, enterprises 262, exchange 300,

301, farm 169, 171, 178, federal 256, federal level 274, federalism 279, fire house 289, formation 256, free trade 255, grid 169, heritage 41, hospital 289, humble 108, independence 256, individual 263, individual investment 212, institution 217, institutional funding 218, institutions 216, intimacy 278, investment 196, 197, 215, 262, law 272, law applied to streets 272, local pleasures 224, management of streets and utilities 275, medical care 175, medical school 175, medical staff 230, merit civil service 178, militia 289, 295, militia obviates police 289, money supply 217, 218, 220, new needs of 278, number of colleges 197, number of wards 179, 182, official knowledge 177, police as occupying force 277, preservation of domain and sovereignty 279, professionalism of, compare to colleges 225, property 214, provision 249, public works 175, religion 180, reserves 179, resources 179, 219, 333, respects transients 168, revenue 217, root polis 171, 219, science 176, seeks only improvements from outside 255, services 172, shared resources 169, shares 196, 215, stewardship 179, stock exchange 219, stock market 221-223, supplies early and loyal customers and workers 214, sustainable union of colleges 249, transient communities in 168, trespass 279, urban 143, utilities 171, 290, wages 229, wall 171, ward 275, 279, water 169

Ward
    character of 276

www.ingramcontent.com/pod-product-compliance
Lightning Source LLC
Chambersburg PA
CBHW032146080426
42735CB00008B/598